MW00715723

Aging
in
Alberta

Rhetoric and Reality
Second Edition

Herbert C. Northcott

Detselig Enterprises Ltd.

Calgary, Alberta, Canada

Aging in Alberta: Rhetoric and Reality, Second Edition
© 1997 Herbert C. Northcott

Canadian Cataloguing in Publication Data

Northcott, Herbert C., 1947-
  Aging in Alberta

Includes bibliographical references.
ISBN 1-55059-135-5

1. Aged—Alberta. I. Title
HQ1064.C2N67   1996   305.26'097123   C96-910179-1

Detselig Enterprises Ltd.
210, 1220 Kensington Rd. N.W.
Calgary, Alberta T2N 3P5

Detselig Enterprises Ltd. appreciates the financial support for our 1997 publishing program, provided by Canadian Heritage and the Alberta Foundation for the Arts, a beneficiary of the Lottery Fund of the Government of Alberta.

All rights reserved. No part of this book may be reproduced in any form or by any means without permission in writing from the publisher.

Printed in Canada

ISBN 1-55059-135-5

SAN 115-0324

Cover design by Dean Macdonald.

Acknowledgments

The author gratefully acknowledges the support of the Public Health Division of Alberta Health, which made the writing of the first edition of this monograph possible. The views expressed are the author's and do not necessarily reflect the official policies of Alberta Health. I am indebted to Mary Engelmann, formerly Director of the Senior Citizens Secretariat, who provided the initial inspiration for this project. The Alberta Health libraries, Family and Social Services library, and particularly the library at the Senior Citizens Secretariat (now at the Seniors Advisory Council for Alberta) have been most helpful. I am particularly grateful to Ted Giles, President of Detselig Enterprises, for his continuing support of this book.

Contents

Foreword vii

1 The Social Construction of the Problem of
Population Aging 9

The Social Construction of Reality and the Political Economy of
Population Aging

Overview

2 The Demography of Aging 15

The Mechanics of Population Aging

Population Aging in the Canadian Context
Return to High Fertility
Increases in the Older Population's Death Rates
Changes in Migration Patterns

Population Aging in Alberta
Distribution of Seniors
Age Structures and Life Expectancies
Sex Ratio
Marital Status
Living Arrangements
Socio-economic Status
Aboriginal Seniors
The Labor Force

Summary

3 The Social Epidemiology of Aging 41

Changing Patterns of Mortality

Changing Patterns of Morbidity

Utilization of Health Care Services by Elderly Albertans

Surveys of Seniors in Provinces Other Than Alberta

Surveys of Seniors in Alberta
National Surveys
Provincial Surveys

Surveys of Seniors in Edmonton
Surveys of Seniors in Calgary
Surveys of Seniors in Northern Alberta
Surveys of Seniors in Central Alberta
Surveys of Seniors in Southern Alberta
Conclusions Arising from the Surveys of Elderly Albertans

4 Issues in Population Aging **67**
Political Issues Associated with Population Aging
    Voting-bloc Scenario
    Equity Scenario
    Summary

Economic Issues Associated with Population Aging
    Bankruptcy Scenario
    Improving-Economic-Situation Scenario
    Less-for-More Scenario
    Add-On Scenario
    Volunteer Scenario
    Shortages of Services in Rural Areas Scenario
    Redefinition-of-Old-Age Scenario
    Summary

Public Attitudes and the Aging of the Population
    Stereotypes and Agism
    Rising Expectations Scenario
    The "I Would Rather Die" Scenario
    The Family Care versus Institutional Care Dilemma
    Attitudes in Alberta
    Summary

Social Ideology and the Aging of the Population
    The Individualism versus Collectivism Paradox
    Holistic Health Promotion Theme
    Summary

5 Issues in Service Delivery **81**
The Development of Health Care Insurance Programs

The Development of Income Security Programs for Seniors

The Philosophical Underpinnings of Canada's Income-Security
and Health-Care Programs

A Review of Selected Policy-Oriented Documents
    The WHO Definition of Health
    The Lalonde Report: A New Perspective
    Achieving Health for All
    Aging: Shifting the Emphasis
    Moving Into the Future: For the Health of Albertans
    Caring and Responsibility
    A New Vision for Long Term Care
    Home Care in Alberta: New Directions in Community Support
    Budget '94: Securing Alberta's Future
    Healthy Albertans Living in a Healthy Alberta: A Three-Year Business Plan
    Government of Alberta Strategic Business Plan for Alberta Seniors 1996/97 to 1998/99
    The Seniors Benefit: Securing the Future
Conclusion

6 Rhetoric and Reality **103**
The Political Economy of Aging in Alberta
    The Fiscal Crisis and Intergenerational Equity
Myth and the Social Construction of Reality in Alberta
    The Future of Population Aging in Alberta

Notes **119**

References **121**

Foreword

Throughout the developed world, increases in life expectancy coupled with declines in fertility have resulted in the aging, or the so-called greying, of populations. That is, in developed countries, seniors (usually defined as persons aged 65 or older) tend to constitute an increasing proportion of a given population. This aging-of-the-population trend has been widely described as a "challenge," a "problem," and/or as a "crisis." In this book, I argue that the crisis definition of population aging is a social construction that in many ways misrepresents and distorts the realities of the population aging trend. I attempt to distinguish the rhetoric of population aging from the realities of population aging. That is, the considerable rhetoric surrounding the aging-of-the-population trend is challenged and scrutinized, and underlying assumptions, veiled motivations, and implications are laid bare.

First, I examine the demography of population aging in Alberta. Then I go on to examine the social epidemiology of aging in Alberta, focusing on rates of service utilization and on local population surveys designed to assess need for services. Various political, economic, and socio-cultural issues associated with population aging and emerging themes in service delivery are then discussed. I argue that the perception of a population aging problem (or crisis) is a social construction that reflects myth more than reality. Further, I argue that the social construction of the population aging problem is fundamentally motivated by economic factors (e.g., fiscal recession) and by various vested interests, rather than by demographic trends, per se.

Chapter One
The Social Construction of the Problem of Population Aging

Population aging, that is, the increase in the proportion of the population that is made up of older persons, is a common demographic phenomenon in the developing and developed countries of the world. This "aging of the population" trend tends to be viewed with some alarm as attempts are made to anticipate and adjust to the social, political, and economic implications of an aging society. In other words, population aging tends to be defined as a social "problem" and reality and rhetoric frequently become intertwined.

The term "rhetoric" is defined in Webster's Dictionary as "the art or science of using words effectively in speaking or writing, so as to influence or persuade." The implication is that rhetoric embodies a degree of artificiality and a certain disregard for the truth. The primary purpose of rhetoric is to motivate and to convince rather than to inform. It is my thesis that there tends to be a great deal of rhetoric associated with discussions of the aging of the population. This rhetoric expresses the anxiety that many have regarding the changes and uncertainties implied by the population aging trend. This rhetoric also serves to express and defend the various points of view of those groups interested in population aging, including the current cohort of seniors, future cohorts of seniors, the labor force, employers, taxpayers, governments, service providers, caregivers, and so on. In other words, various interest groups tend to have differing perceptions of the population aging phenomenon and tend to select those facts and arguments that best serve their vested interests. It is the purpose of this monograph to examine population aging in the province of Alberta and to attempt to separate rhetoric from reality.

One could ask: Why study Alberta? In comparison to the nine other Canadian provinces, Alberta has the lowest proportion of seniors in its population. Nevertheless, there is considerable concern in Alberta, as there is elsewhere in Canada, over the population aging trend. In other words, Alberta merits study because in this province rhetoric and reality may be particularly discrepant.

There is an old sociological saying which states that whatever people think is real will be real in its consequences (Spencer, 1985:142 – attributed to W.I. Thomas). In the physical world, an imaginary cause cannot have a real effect. However, human beings are not wholly constrained by the physical laws of nature and those things that people imagine can have real consequences. This is a process that social scientists have called the social construction of reality (for a book of this title, see Berger and Luckmann, 1966). That is, individuals, groups, and societies tend to place interpretations upon reality – interpretations which may or may not be true in an absolute sense. These definitions, explanations, and assertions are constructed to help us make sense of those things and events that we experience and to help us decide how to respond to those experiences. In the face of uncertainty and ambiguity, these social constructions provide definition and direction. However, these social constructions themselves are frequently based on "fashionable" and therefore changeable assumptions and value judgments.

Let me illustrate the above argument with several examples from the health literature. The use of tobacco, when first introduced into European society, was considered a filthy and disgusting practice. In time, chewing, sniffing, and smoking tobacco became quite widely accepted, for males at least, and, indeed, favorably defined. Consider Sherlock Holmes with his pipe, the aristocrat with his snuff, the businessman with his cigar, the cowboy with his "chew," and James Dean with his cigarette. Tobacco, variously used, became part of a person's social image – part of a person's attempt to create a favorable definition of himself, and later of herself, both in the eyes of others and in his/her own eyes. Today, of course, the use of tobacco has been redefined once again and is now perceived to be a major health risk, and increasingly, a socially offensive practice.

As another example, consider the definition of a healthy diet. Meat, dairy products, eggs, and refined flour were once our dietary staples. Then came warnings about the dangers of cholesterol, fats, the absence of fibre, and so on. More recently, we hear that these food products may not be all that bad, and indeed may be good in moderation, or that the problem may not be so much in what we eat but in how our body processes our daily diet. My point is that these various expert pronouncements seem to the person in the street to have undergone recent and relatively rapid change reflecting both an evolving knowledge base and changing assumptions and values.

As a final example, consider the jogging and aerobics health craze. A decade ago, when it seemed that everybody was jogging and working out, it was easy to believe that our society had reached a new and permanent definition of the route to perfect health. But again, our definitions seem to be changing as our attention shifts to gentler forms of recreation and, perhaps more significantly, as our attention shifts from personal lifestyle issues to environmental issues. We seem to be more and more concerned these days with the quality of the environment in which we collectively live. Today, the pressing issues are air quality, water quality, hazardous waste disposal, and recycling.

To put this argument differently, what is perceived as a social problem one day may be seen in quite different terms or forgotten on another day. And vice versa – yesterday's complacencies may become tomorrow's problems. On the one hand, these changing definitions reflect advances in knowledge and technology leading to solutions to old problems and the creation of new problems. On the other hand, society's changing definitions of its social concerns reflect more than problem-solving. These definitions also reflect, for lack of a better word, "fashion."

This monograph addresses a contemporary and fashionable social "problem," namely the aging of the population in Canada in general and in Alberta in particular. This current issue is related to another social problem that was very much on the public's mind several decades ago. At that time, there was considerable energy and concern invested in a social phenomenon referred to as the "population explosion." When one heard discussions or read the literature on this issue (see, for example, Ehrlich, 1968), one's anxiety rose and one felt a sense of urgency that this problem must be solved before it was too late, before the human race overpopulated the earth and destroyed itself. Since then, the baby boom has ended in Western nations and the birth rate has dropped in many parts of the world. Nevertheless, the birth rate is still relatively high in many countries and the human population still continues to increase. I am making two points: first, the solution to yesterday's problem often is the cause of today's problem. That is, the solution to the population explosion – lowering birth rates – has caused the aging of the population. Second, while the population explosion phenomenon still continues to a degree in parts of the world, the concern felt by people generally about this problem seems to have been forgotten. Or rather, concern seems to have shifted to the more fashionable and current "problem" – population aging. Now, one could ask if the concern over the population explosion was really warranted, that is, was there ever really a problem? The answer to that question depends on your point of view and, of course, benefits from hindsight. Similarly, one could ask whether the current concern over the aging of the population is warranted. It is the purpose of this book to address this very question, exploring various points of view on this issue.

I am suggesting that population aging is a socially constructed, fashionable, social problem. Reality lies shrouded in ambiguity and rhetoric – ambiguity because we can only guess the future and rhetoric because the media and social critics have a vested interest in calling attention to social issues and in cultivating public anxiety. This is not all bad. We do need to anticipate future problems so that we can deal with them before they get out of hand. Nevertheless, we do need to sort the reality from the rhetoric. This is no easy task, given that our social problems are defined and resolved in ongoing public and political debates over values. That is, there is no way of defining social reality in absolute terms. Science can discover the ultimate truths of the physical universe. Science, however, cannot ultimately resolve questions of value. Such questions are addressed in public forums, in churches, legislatures, and courts. Once a consensus is defined, science may be called upon to implement or evaluate the chosen solution. Nevertheless, it follows that our social problems will always embody both rhetoric and reality.

The Social Construction of Reality and the Political Economy of Population Aging

Marshall (1987a:52-54) states that the political economy perspective is favored by many Canadian social scientists engaged in the study of population aging (see, for example, Leonard and Nichols, 1994; Myles, 1989; Myles and

Teichroew, 1991). The political economy perspective identifies the various groups that have an interest in an issue and examines the definitions, symbols, and ideologies used by these groups in the pursuit of their interests. Referring to analyses of the 1982 United Nations World Assembly on Aging (see Shapiro and Kaufert, 1983; Neysmith and Edwardh, 1983), Marshall (1987a:53) observes that such government-sponsored conferences "use experts to promote definitions of the social problems of the aged that ignore substantive issues [regarding] the economic and social marginalization of the aged . . . and legitimate token gestures to the aged and band-aid solutions to their problems." Shapiro and Kaufert (1983), in their analysis of the process leading up to and including the 1982 World Assembly on Aging, argue that politicians, policy-makers, bureaucrats, scientific and technical experts, professionals, and so on often share common backgrounds and perspectives. Further, these persons have vested interests in protecting and enhancing their status and achieving career objectives. For these reasons, such persons may become "part of a symbolic process which legitimates the definitions of 'social problems' and the policy responses of national governments" (p. 44). At the same time, this process validates the roles of these policy-makers, bureaucrats, and experts. Even small groups of laypersons (appointed to committees, for example) may be co-opted so that governments can maintain the appearance of having consulted "the people" who will actually be affected by definitions of problems and the resulting policies. In other words, the definition of the "problem" and the proposed solutions may serve the vested interests of the problem definers and policy-makers, but have little relevance to those persons who are the object of discussion. Indeed, defining a group (of seniors, for example) and their concerns as a "problem" tends to "blame the victim" (i.e., seniors themselves come to be seen as "the problem") and obscures the need for fundamental social (i.e., structural) change.

Estes, in the United States, makes a similar argument (Estes, et al., 1982). Estes (1979; 1983; 1984; 1991; Estes, et al., 1984) examined the 1965 Older Americans Act (and subsequent amendments), the resulting Administration on Aging, the Social Security "crisis" of the early 1980s, American health care policy as it relates to seniors, and fiscal austerity and its implications for old age and public policy. Estes argues that public policies tend to reflect and serve the interests of dominant social, political, and economic groups. These interest groups construct and manipulate definitions of reality which justify self-serving policies. For example, Estes argues that the "aging crisis" in the United States is a social construction that serves politicians, bureaucrats, and service providers more than it benefits seniors. The crisis definition of the situation justifies allocation of funds to government and service agencies (benefitting the agencies as much as the clients served by these agencies) and justifies "sacrifice" on the part of others. More insidiously, Estes argues, various vested interests in the service economy engaged in the "aging enterprise" profit from the servicing of seniors, while seniors are made dependent, stigmatized, exploited, benefitted too little, and ultimately blamed for the aging crisis. In short, the victim-blaming ideology is used to deflect attention away from policies which justify the service providers and legitimate their exploitation of seniors and of tax dollars. In sum,

Estes argues that humanitarian claims of "helping" the aged hide the fact that powerful interest groups are, first and foremost, helping themselves.

Guillemard (1983; see also Guallier, 1982) uses a similar approach in her analysis of changing definitions (she refers to these as "social reconstructions") of old age and old age policies in France since the Second World War. In short, she argues that these shifts in definitions and policy are influenced by the relationships between the state and various social and economic interests. Similarly, Walker (1981; 1983; 1991; see also Townsend, 1981), focusing on Great Britain, argues that the dependency of seniors has been socially engineered and constitutes a "structurally enforced inferior social and economic status" (1983:144). While the contemporary welfare state provides certain benefits to seniors, nevertheless, many disadvantages come with this socially created and enforced dependency status. Walker suggests that the disadvantages to seniors outweigh the advantages, and that, in any case, aging policies reflect the interests of various economic and political groups more than they reflect the interests of seniors.

In summary, the social construction of reality and political economy perspectives, as applied to the study of population aging, suggest that the current population aging "problem" or "crisis" is socially defined, i.e., socially constructed. This definition of seniors and seniors' issues reflects various dominant social, political, and economic interests. While the crisis definition may be misleading, and while the "facts" may indeed suggest alternative definitions of the situation, researchers argue that the crisis definition persists because it serves the interests of certain groups in society.

Overview

The following chapter examines the demography of population aging. I discuss the demographic determinants of population aging – fertility, mortality, and migration. Following a brief discussion of the international and national context, I examine population aging in Alberta in detail and present the geographic distribution of seniors (rural-urban, north-south) in Alberta. I examine trends in life expectancies and age-sex structures and, in addition, review the marital status, living arrangements, and socio-economic status of seniors in Alberta. Native seniors and, finally, trends in the labor force are also discussed.

In Chapter 3, I examine the social epidemiology of aging, focusing on changing patterns of morbidity and mortality. I discuss the utilization of health care services by elderly Albertans and review surveys examining the needs of seniors in Alberta.

I discuss political and economic issues, public attitudes, and emerging social ideologies related to population aging in Chapter 4. The implications of broad societal trends for future service delivery are discussed. In the fifth chapter, I examine the development of health-care and income-security programs for seniors and discuss the philosophical underpinnings of these programs. I analyze selected policy statements in order to examine emerging directions in health care and other services for seniors.

The final chapter is a return to the theme of rhetoric and reality. I argue that the population aging phenomenon and its implications are obscured by rhetoric, myth, and misperception. I attempt to separate rhetoric from reality.

Chapter Two
The Demography of Aging

Population aging refers to an increase in the proportion of the population that is seniors, defined somewhat arbitrarily as persons 60 or 65 years of age and older. According to the United Nations (see Novak, 1993:69), a society is "young" if less than 4% of its population is seniors (60+ years of age) and is "aged" when that figure reaches 10%. According to these criteria, Alberta became an aged province shortly after the Second World War. However, before examining population aging in Alberta, it is useful to briefly examine population aging around the world so that the study of Alberta can be put into context.

Table 2.1 lists a number of regions and countries around the world, showing that the developed nations have the highest percentages of seniors aged 65 and older. Europe, with 14% seniors, is the "oldest" region in the world. Indeed, Sweden has a higher percentage of seniors (17%) than any other country. North America (the United States and Canada) is comparable to Europe with 13% seniors. Asia has a much lower percentage of seniors than North America, nevertheless, Asia's "oldest" country is Japan, which has 15% seniors. Oceania's "oldest" countries are Australia and New Zealand, both tied with Canada at 12% seniors. While Latin America has a few countries with relatively high percentages of seniors, the region as a whole is quite "youthful." The region of the world with the lowest percentage of seniors is Africa. Differences among countries and regions of the world are substantial. Compare Europe at 14% to Africa at 3% or Sweden's 17% to Mozambique's 2%.

The Mechanics of Population Aging

Population aging in Alberta and elsewhere is primarily a function of birth and death rates, although migration can also have an effect. Historically, societies have tended to have high birth and high death rates. Many people were born, but many died, often at a very young age. Despite the high birth rate, the high death rate usually meant that the population increased in size only at a modest rate, if at all. Further, because of the high birth rate and low average life expectancy, the average age of the population was low and elders made up a relatively small percentage of the population. With improvements in the standard of living and the development of modern medicine, death rates tend to drop and average life expectancy increases. Birth rates, supported by culturally-based value systems, tend to remain high for a time. Because more and more babies survive infancy and early childhood, the population remains youthful in terms of age composition but begins to grow rapidly in size.

Table 2.1
Percentage of Population 65 Years of Age and Older for Regions of the World, 1996
(with selected "older" countries)

Region or Country	Percentage of Population 65+ Years of Age	
World	6	
Europe	14	
–Sweden		17
–Belgium		16
–Italy		16
–Norway		16
–United Kingdom		16
North America (excluding Latin America)	13	
–United States		13
–Canada		12
Oceania	10	
–Australia		12
–New Zealand		12
Asia	5	
–Japan		15
–Georgia		10
–Hong Kong		9
Latin America	5	
–Barbados		12
–Uruguay		12
–Puerto Rico		10
–Argentina		9
Africa	3	
–Seychelles		7
–Mauritius		6

Source: Adapted from Population Reference Bureau,
1996 World Population Data Sheet

This defines the so-called "population explosion" – high birth rates, declining death rates, and a high rate of growth. In time, birth rates also tend to begin to fall as individual and collective perceptions and definitions regarding reproductive behavior change. As the birth rate falls, the rate of population growth begins to decline and the percentage of the population that is aged begins to increase. With relatively fewer and fewer babies being born, and with more and more persons living to an advanced age, it follows that the average age in the population and also the percentage of the population that is aged will increase. This process of moving from high to low birth and death rates is known as the demographic transition. Note that if birth and death rates stabilize, this period of transition will end in time. Let me emphasize this point. While the period of demographic transition will see the world's human population increase substantially in number and will see the aged percentage of the population increase significantly, nevertheless, the explosion-of-the-population trend and the later aging-of-the-population trend will both cease, if birth and death rates stabilize at low levels.

The demographic transition describes a process that has been typical of developing nations. Of course, however typical this process has been, it is not inevitable. In the future, birth rates might remain high in developing countries or rebound in developed nations. Alternatively, death rates might rise again at some time in the future. Rising birth and/or death rates would tend to offset or even reverse population aging. In other words, it is possible to describe alternative scenarios for the future.

In the most common scenario, it is assumed that the developed nations will continue with low birth rates and low death rates. Such a population would have a near zero rate of growth (ranging from modest rates of population decline to modest rates of growth) and, eventually, a relatively stable although high proportion of aged. In this scenario it is usually assumed that underdeveloped and developing nations will sooner or later undergo the demographic transition and become demographically similar to today's developed nations.

While it is usually assumed that high birth rates will decline (most countries today with high birth rates seek to bring those rates down and modernization tends to be associated with falling or low rates of birth), it is also possible that births will remain high and perhaps possible, although unlikely, that these rates could even rise. Similarly, while it is usually assumed that low birth rates will remain low, it is possible that rates will decline even further and also possible that these rates will rebound. Given that very low birth rates are associated with declines in the size of the population and in the labor force, some jurisdictions have begun to see low rates of birth as a social problem. And so the pendulum swings! First, high birth rates are a problem and then low birth rates are. Among developed countries today, some (e.g., France, Bulgaria, Hungary, and the former Czechoslovakia) have adopted pronatalist policies to stem declines in population size (Romaniuc, 1984:24, 101-105). The province of Quebec, concerned about the decline in the proportion of Francophones in the Canadian population, has also adopted policies designed to encourage a higher birth rate (Romaniuc, 1984:101; Maclean's, May 30, 1988). Generally speaking, a low or falling *birth* rate implies an aged or aging population while a high or rising *birth* rate implies a youthful population or a population that is becoming more youthful.

While it is usually assumed that death rates will decline as standards of living improve, it is also possible that death rates could rise. While we tend to take an optimistic view of prospects for future declines in mortality, nevertheless, death rates could rise for any of a number of reasons, including either natural or man-made environmental catastrophes, new and deadly biological diseases, socio-political disasters such as nuclear warfare, or socio-economic collapse in the world economy. Nevertheless, it is generally expected that death rates will fall, assuming improvements in lifestyles, living environments, and medical advances. Should medical science unlock the biogenetic keys to the human aging process, a significant lowering of the death rate would be possible. Currently, this alternative remains a topic more for science fiction, although several generations ago science fiction contemplated wonderful dreams (e.g., space flight) that have since come true. Generally speaking, a low or falling *death* rate implies an aged or aging population while a high or rising *death* rate implies a youthful population or a population that is becoming more youthful.

Table 2.2 summarizes the effects of birth and death rates on the age structure of the population. It should be noted that this discussion is illustrative only and over-simplifies reality for several reasons. First, no trend occurs in isolation. Birth rates, death rates, and migration patterns all combine to influence the course of population aging. Second, I have ignored the phenomenon of demographic momentum. One of the most salient momentum features of contemporary Canadian society is the baby boom, which is the result of high fertility following the Second World War. That is, past levels of fertility are still having a demographic effect on our society and will continue to do so for some time.

Table 2.2
An Illustrative Typology Showing the Effects of Various Birth and Death Rates on Population Age Structure and on Population Aging

Birth and Death Rate		Population Age Structure	
Rate	Trend	Age Composition	Aging Trend
Birth Rate			
High	Rising	Young	More Youthful
High	Stable	Young	Stable
High	Falling	Young	Aging
Low	Rising	Old	More Youthful
Low	Stable	Old	Stable
Low	Falling	Old	Aging
Death Rate			
High	Rising	Young	More Youthful
High	Stable	Young	Stable
High	Falling	Young	Aging
Low	Rising	Old	More Youthful
Low	Stable	Old	Stable
Low	Falling	Old	Aging

Up to this point, I have not discussed the effects of migration on population aging. Of course, the in-migration of seniors enhances population aging while the out-migration of the aged reduces the aged proportion. It is also true that the migration of non-seniors affects population aging. The out-migration of young people means that the older folks left behind will make up an increasing proportion of the remaining population. Alternatively, the in-migration of young people will dilute the seniors' presence and reduce their proportion in the population. Further, these patterns can combine to counter-balance each other. Table 2.3 summarizes these effects. Usually, the migration rates for the younger age groups exceed the migration rates for the older age groups. As a consequence, when both old and young are moving into a given area, there is a tendency for proportionately more young persons to come, making the population less aged. Where both old and young are moving away from a given area, young persons will tend to leave at a greater rate, increasing the proportion of seniors in the remaining population.

Table 2.3
An Illustrative Typology Showing the Effects of Migration on Population Aging

Age-Specific Migration Pattern	Population Aging Trend
1. In-Migration of Young	More Youthful
2. Out-Migration of Old	More Youthful
3. Out-Migration of Young	More Aged
4. In-Migration of Old	More Aged
Combinations:	
1 and 2	More Youthful
1 and 4	Usually More Youthful
2 and 3	Usually More Aged
3 and 4	More Aged

Population Aging in the Canadian Context

Up to this point I have been discussing the determinants of population aging in very general terms. Let me turn now to a discussion of aging in the Canadian context. (For a comprehensive "fact book" on aging in Canada, see Elliot, 1996.)

While public attention in Canada has only recently focused on the aging of the population, Canada has been "aging" for many decades now and is expected to continue to age well into the twenty-first century. In 1881, Canada had just over 4% of its population aged 65 and older. By 1971, this figure had doubled to 8.1%. (See McDaniel, 1986:36 and Beaujot, 1991:206 for trend data from 1851 to 1986.) The 1991 census placed the elderly proportion of the Canadian population at 11.6% (Norland, 1994).

Population aging in Canada has been a function of death rates that have been falling throughout the twentieth century, and birth rates that have fallen dramatically since the post-war baby boom high. The effects of migration patterns on population aging are not as clear. On the one hand, migration into Canada has tended to be disproportionately younger adults and this movement tends to offset the population aging process. On the other hand, migration out of Canada (mostly to the United States) has also been substantial and has also favored younger adults, a pattern that contributes to population aging within Canada.

Canada is expected to age well into the twenty-first century, with the elderly percentage of the population peaking in the low to mid-twenties sometime around the end of the first third of the twenty-first century (McDaniel, 1986:106; Denton, et al., 1986; Beaujot, 1991:203; Statistics Canada, 1994a:vi, 72-73, 81). These projections regarding the future percentage of seniors in the population are based on **assumptions** regarding future patterns of fertility, mortality, and migration. These projections tend to show that, of these three variables, the single most important cause of population aging in Canada is expected to be the fertility rate (McDaniel, 1986:6, 9, 94, 104; Denton, et al., 1986:84; Beaujot, 1991:207-208; Statistics Canada, 1994a:7; McVey and Kalbach, 1995:75-76). Further, the population aging process in Canada will be augmented for a period of time by the aging of the baby boom. If the baby boom is defined as those persons born during the post-war census periods from 1946 to 1966 (Stone and Fletcher, 1986: Section 1.1; Statistics Canada, 1994a:vi), then the seniors boom will begin in 2011 (1946+65) and begin to wind down in 2031.

Given the current concern over the aging of the Canadian population, it is useful to consider demographic strategies that might be implemented to avoid attaining the forecasted proportions of seniors. There are several options, including a return to high fertility, increases in the older population's death rates, and changes in migration patterns (that is, increases in the in-migration of younger adults, and increases in the out-migration of older adults). These will be discussed individually.

Return to High Fertility

There are several ways in which Canadians or Albertans **might** be enticed to produce more children. Consider, for example, a public education campaign designed to highlight the central role of low fertility in the aging process and designed to show that today's babies in two to three decades would become wage earners and taxpayers in time to guarantee the pensions of the forthcoming seniors boom. Or consider governmental incentives, including substantially increased tax deductions and/or tax credits for children, cash payments for third and fourth and subsequent children, a homemaker's pension, a national day care system, and so on. Nevertheless, attempts by government to raise the birth rate are likely to have little, if any, effect (Romaniuc, 1984:24, 105-110), although it is conceivable that having children might become **socially** fashionable again at some time in the future.

Increases in the Older Population's Death Rates

Another strategy that can theoretically be applied as a solution for the aging "problem" involves raising seniors' death rates. This, of course, is virtually unthinkable. We are not about to pass the hemlock to each citizen who turns 65 years of age or any other age for that matter. However, consider the relatively high rates of elder suicide, especially for males (Health Canada, 1994:22; Health and Welfare Canada, 1987a; 1982) and the possibility of these rates rising. Consider such notions as the living will[1] (see Alberta Health, 1994a; Alberta Law Reform Institute, 1993; Alberta Senior Citizens Secretariat, 1985), palliative care, concern over the quality of life as opposed to the quantity of life, the right to die, assisted suicide, and euthanasia (see the Special Senate Committee on Euthanasia and Assisted Suicide, 1995; Ogden, 1994). Should such ideas and practices become commonplace (fashionable?), then the substantial costs of caring for the terminally ill might be reduced somewhat. However, these possibilities are unlikely to have a significant effect on the proportion of elderly persons in the population.

Changes in Migration Patterns

Other possible strategies for offsetting the aging trend involve migration patterns. Canada is relatively sparsely populated (as is Alberta) and self-sufficient in food production and could therefore sustain a larger population. Canada might encourage in-migration through greatly expanded immigration quotas and through economic incentives offered to immigrants. While migration tends to be selective for younger adults and families generally, nevertheless, Canada's migration policy might specifically state preferences for these younger adult age groups and for persons from cultures that favor high birth rates, so that for a generation or two at least, these new Canadians might also contribute to a higher birth rate. However, such massive in-migration tends to be disruptive socially, politically, and economically, and it is unlikely that migration will be encouraged on this scale. A rather different kind of in-migration strategy involves the importation of children from other countries for adoption in Canada. Such a strategy might appeal to some degree to Canadian families who want to adopt children; however, such a strategy might also encourage the development of an international "trade" in babies. Again, such a "solution" seems rather far-fetched.

Out-migration might also be manipulated in an attempt to deal with the population aging process. For example, Canada might attempt to reduce or control out-migration of its younger population either by making Canada relatively more attractive to its labor force than the United States (the principal destination) or by closing its borders. Alternatively, the population aging process is also offset by the out-migration of seniors. We know that many elderly Canadians spend significant proportions of the winter months in the United States (the so-called "snowbirds"). This seasonal migration by itself, of course, is not a solution to the aging phenomenon. The snowbirds are but extended vacationers who return home to Canada, many to preserve their medicare coverage. Perhaps ways could be found to facilitate the permanent migration of seniors to warmer climates or to countries with lower costs of living. Nevertheless, Canada's health care system will remain a powerful disincentive for such movement. Neither restricting the out-migration of young people nor encouraging the out-migration of seniors seems very plausible.

Finally, the above discussion assumes that there is a group of people – seniors – who are identifiable as such. While human societies have long recognized the signs of physiological aging, old age as a social category is a social construction (Green, 1993). Indeed, the idea of a category of senior citizens defined by age (e.g., 65+), excluded from the labor force by retirement practices, and supported from the public purse (through pensions, old age security payments, and so on) is a relatively recent twentieth century development in Western nations (Myles, 1984; 1989). If we, as a society, have created old age through rather arbitrary definitions and public policy, then in the same manner we can redefine old age or even define it away. The 1982 Canadian Charter of Rights and Freedoms (see Section 15(1)), which forbids discrimination on the basis of age, may be but one of the forces which might undermine our present definitions of old age and related social policies.[2] In other words, it can be argued that mandatory retirement (for a discussion of issues, see Guppy, 1989) or waiver of health care premiums for seniors are agist social policies that express negative stereotypes about a segment of our population and institutionalize discriminatory practices that disadvantage or advantage that social group.

Agism, like sexism and racism, is coming under increasing scrutiny and is increasingly under attack on humanitarian grounds. Alternatively, it can be argued that the social construction of the senior citizen group, of retirement policy, and of pension and old age security systems was motivated by the vested interests of employers and younger age groups who benefitted from the displacement of seniors from the labor force (Myles, 1984; 1989; McDonald and Wanner, 1990). When the elderly age group made up a relatively small percentage of the population, employers and younger age groups could afford to offer seniors the enticements of a paid retirement, not, you understand, out of the goodness of their hearts, but out of a desire for personal gain. As the number and proportion of seniors have risen and as their expectations have also risen, the cost of supporting the retired population is perceived to be increasingly problematic. Society, in the near future, may claim to see the error of its ways and may express a desire to implement a more humane approach to old age. That is, society, once again under the guise of humanitarian concern, may do away with old age as a social category and with mandatory retirement. Under this somewhat cynical interpretation, the vested interests of employers and younger age groups are once again served by social policy, and as before, under the pretense of serving the older age group.

Whether you think mandatory retirement and the attendant definitions of old age are good or bad, my point is that one way of dealing with the social "problem" of population aging is to simply define it away. Assuming that such redefinitions also do away with entitlements based solely on age (e.g., old age security), then society's burden of supporting its aged population is reduced. Such redefinitions might even have a modest impact on the health care costs incurred by seniors. For example, all seniors in Alberta, until 1994, were exempted from paying health care premiums. Changing definitions of old age might well affect patterns of health care utilization and might also be associated with changes in the mechanisms of and responsibility for payment.

Population Aging in Alberta

Let me now turn to a discussion of population aging in the province of Alberta. Table 2.4 shows that Alberta is the "youngest" province in Canada, having the lowest proportion of seniors. Only the Yukon and Northwest Territories have lower proportions. Differences in provincial levels and rates of population aging are a result of differentials (past and present) in birth rates, death rates, international migration patterns, and interprovincial migration patterns. Saskatchewan is one of the oldest provinces in Canada primarily because there has been a significant out-flow of young adults from that province, leaving a relatively high concentration of senior citizens in the remaining population. Now, seniors have also moved in significant numbers from Saskatchewan, the majority going to British Columbia and Alberta (Northcott, 1988a:57-58). Nevertheless, the rate of non-elderly out-migration exceeds the rate of elderly out-migration, resulting in a relatively high proportion of seniors. Similarly, Alberta's relative "youthfulness" is explained to a significant degree by migration between provinces. In the oil boom years of the 1970s, Alberta attracted many young adults, and while some left the province following the 1982 recession, many stayed, and of course, many of these new Albertans are now raising families. These patterns tended to offset the trend toward population aging; indeed, in the 1976-1981 period, Alberta was the only province in Canada that got younger instead of older in terms of the elderly percentage of the population. While the outmigration following the 1982 recession contributed to Alberta's population aging during the 1981-1986 period, nevertheless, Alberta remains the youngest province in Canada. I will now discuss the distribution of seniors within Alberta and examine future projections.

Table 2.4
The Percentage of the Canadian Population Which is Seniors,
by Province, 1991, 1986, and 1981

	Percentage 65 Years of Age and Older		
Province	1991	1986	1981
Newfoundland	9.7	8.8	7.7
Prince Edward Island	13.2	12.7	12.2
Nova Scotia	12.6	11.9	10.9
New Brunswick	12.2	11.1	10.1
Quebec	11.2	10.0	8.8
Ontario	11.7	10.9	10.1
Manitoba	13.4	12.6	11.9
Saskatchewan	14.1	12.7	12.0
Alberta	9.1	8.1	7.3
British Columbia	12.9	12.1	10.9
Yukon Territory	4.0	3.7	3.2
Northwest Territories	2.8	2.8	2.9
Canada	**11.6**	**10.7**	**9.7**

Source: Adapted from Statistics Canada. 1991 Census of Canada,
Catalogue Number 93-310, Table 1

Table 2.5
The Percentage of the Population 65 Years of Age and Older and 75 Years of Age
and Older in Alberta Census Divisions and Major Cities, 1991

Census Divisions (and Major Cities)	65 Years of Age and Older		75 Years of Age and Older	
	Number	Percentage of Population	Number	Percentage of Population
Alberta	230 550	9.1	93 145	3.7
1	7655	13.2	3100	5.3
(Medicine Hat)	(6435)	(14.8)	(2660)	(6.1)
2	14 365	12.1	6335	5.3
(Lethbridge)	(8455)	(13.9)	(3845)	(6.3)
3	4685	13.0	2130	5.9
4	1650	13.8	635	5.3
5	5000	12.6	2100	5.3
6	64 155	8.0	24 875	3.1
(Calgary)	(56 215)	(7.9)	(21 580)	(3.0)
7	5760	14.5	2490	6.3
8	12 795	10.3	5325	4.3
(Red Deer)	(5095)	(8.8)	(2115)	(3.6)
9	1520	9.1	570	3.4
10	12 480	15.9	5820	7.4
11	74 920	8.5	29 430	3.4
(Edmonton)	(58 745)	(9.5)	(23 235)	(3.8)
12	4080	9.4	1760	4.1
13	7040	12.2	2830	4.9
14	1690	6.6	645	2.5
15	2220	8.4	900	3.4
16	1455	2.9	565	1.1
(Fort McMurray)	(380)	(1.1)	(125)	(0.4)
17	2565	5.2	970	2.0
18	600	4.3	195	1.4
19	5905	7.9	2475	3.3
(Grande Prairie)	(1660)	(5.9)	(735)	(2.6)

Source: Adapted from Statistics Canada. 1991 Census of Canada.
Catalogue Number 95-372.

Table 2.6
The Percentage Distribution of Seniors in Alberta, 1991

Census Divisions (and Major Cities)	Percentage Distribution of Albertans 65 Years of Age and Older	Percentage Distribution of Albertans 75 Years of Age and Older
1 (Medicine Hat)	3.32 (2.79)	3.33 (2.86)
2 (Lethbridge)	6.23 (3.67)	6.80 (4.13)
3	2.03	2.29
4	0.72	0.68
5	2.17	2.25
6 (Calgary)	27.83 (24.38)	26.70 (23.17)
7	2.50	2.67
8 (Red Deer)	5.55 (2.21)	5.72 (2.27)
9	0.66	0.61
10	5.41	6.25
11 (Edmonton)	32.50 (25.48)	31.59 (24.94)
12	1.77	1.89
13	3.05	3.04
14	0.73	0.69
15	0.96	0.97
16 (Fort McMurray)	0.63 (0.16)	0.61 (0.13)
17	1.11	1.04
18	0.26	0.21
19 (Grande Prairie)	2.56 (0.72)	2.66 (0.79)
Total	100.0	100.0

Source: Adapted from Statistics Canada. 1991 Census of Canada.
Catalogue Number 95-372.

There are several ways to subdivide Alberta geographically.[3] Table 2.5 shows the numbers of seniors (65+, 75+) and their percentages of the local population for census divisions and major cities in Alberta. Table 2.6 shows the proportion of the province's seniors that reside in a given census division or city.[4] Half of Alberta's seniors reside in either Edmonton or Calgary; 60% reside in census divisions #6 and #11 that encompass the cities of Edmonton and Calgary. Another 10% of Alberta's seniors reside in either Lethbridge, Medicine Hat, Red Deer, Grande Prairie, or Fort McMurray and almost one-fifth (18%) reside in either these cities or their surrounding census divisions. About one-fifth (21%) of Alberta's seniors reside in a census division that does not contain a major city. Only 9% of older Albertans live in the census divisions north of Edmonton (#12, 13, 16, 17, 18, and 19). The distribution of persons 75+ years of age throughout the province is very similar to the distribution of persons 65+ years of age, suggesting that there are no dramatic displacements of the older old from one census division to another.

Turning now to population projections, Statistics Canada occasionally publishes population projections for Canada, the provinces, and the territories. In 1994, Statistics Canada (1994a) published projections for 1993-2016 using various assumptions about fertility, mortality, immigration, emigration, non-permanent residents, returning Canadians, and interprovincial migration. Table 2.7 shows high, medium, and low growth projections for Alberta. The low growth projections show the percentage of aged rising from 9.8% in 1996 to 14.5% in 2016. (Recall my earlier discussion that states that low population growth tends to be associated with population aging.) In contrast, the high growth projections show the percentage aged rising to 13.4% by 2016.

These projections assume that there will not be dramatic medical breakthroughs that substantially lower death rates and that there will not be dramatic reversals in mortality trends, for example, increases in death rates from new and deadly diseases, from natural disasters, or from man-made disasters such as environmental pollution or warfare. These projections also assume that there will not be massive in- or out-migrations. It is, of course, impossible to predict the future with total accuracy. It is easiest (and often more comfortable psychologically) to assume that trends and patterns will continue more or less as they have in the past. Under the range of assumptions used in the Statistics Canada projections, the percentage of aged should rise over the 20 years from 1996 to 2016 to somewhere between 13 and 15%. Note that these proportions of aged have already been attained or exceeded in a number of European nations (see Table 2.1), are equalled currently in Saskatchewan (14.1% seniors in 1991), and have already been surpassed in cities such as Victoria (18.6% in 1991) or in states such as Florida (18.3% in 1990; U.S. Bureau of the Census, 1991). I will explore the implications of Alberta's relatively modest aging trend in subsequent chapters.

Table 2.7
Projections for Population 65 and Older in Alberta, 1996-2016

Projection Series	Projected Population				
	1996	2001	2006	2011	2016
Low Growth					
Number 65+ (thousands)	273	310	345	395	477
% of Population	9.8	10.6	11.3	12.4	14.5
Medium Growth					
Number 65+ (thousands)	274	313	352	408	497
% of Population	9.8	10.5	11.1	12.2	14.1
High Growth (& west internal migration)					
Number 65+ (thousands)	275	318	364	431	537
% of Population	9.8	10.3	10.8	11.7	13.4

Source: Adapted from Statistics Canada, 1994a, Table A3.

Table 2.8 shows that those seniors who are 85 years of age or older constituted about 1.0% of Albertans in 1996. In 20 years, this statistic may rise to somewhere around 1.8% of the total population.

Table 2.8
Projections for Population 85 and Older in Alberta, 1996-2016

Projection Series	Projected Population				
	1996	2001	2006	2011	2016
Low Growth					
Number 65+ (thousands)	27.7	35.5	43.2	52.0	59.5
% of Population	1.00	1.21	1.41	1.64	1.81
Medium Growth					
Number 65+ (thousands)	27.9	36.0	44.5	54.6	64.0
% of Population	1.00	1.21	1.41	1.63	1.81
High Growth (& west internal migration)					
Number 65+ (thousands)	28.0	37.0	47.3	60.3	73.9
% of Population	1.00	1.20	1.40	1.63	1.84

Source: Adapted from Statistics Canada, 1994a, Table A3.

The Seniors Advisory Council for Alberta produces a document, generally every two years, which examines the demography of population aging in Alberta. I will briefly summarize relevant demographic facts and trends drawing from the Council's 1993 publication,[5] as well as other sources.

Distribution of Seniors

As noted earlier in this chapter, the great majority of Alberta's seniors live in urban areas (about one-half reside in Edmonton and Calgary alone). Indeed, seniors have become increasingly concentrated in urban centres. In 1971, 73% of Alberta's seniors lived in urban areas while 10% lived on the farm, the remainder residing in rural non-farm settings. Twenty years later in 1991, 80% of seniors resided in urban settings while only 5% remained on the farm (Seniors Advisory Council for Alberta, 1993:28). This trend is consistent with the longstanding movement of the population (both elderly and non-elderly) from the countryside to town and city.

Another important dimension in Alberta, besides the rural-urban distinction, is the north-south dimension. The northern half of the province is relatively sparsely populated, and, accordingly, has a relatively small portion of Alberta's total senior population. Indeed, as noted earlier in this chapter, in 1991 only 9% of Alberta's seniors resided in the northern half of the province (i.e., in census divisions north of Edmonton).

There are wide variations in the concentration of seniors throughout the province. In 1991, seniors made up 9.0% of the population of urban centres, 9.9% of the population of rural non-farm areas, but only 6.9% of the farm population (Seniors Advisory Council for Alberta, 1993:31). In 1991, the concentration of seniors ranged in major cities in Alberta from a high of 14.8% in Medicine Hat to a low of 1.1% in Fort McMurray, while the concentration of seniors in census divisions (CDs) ranged from a high of 15.9% in C.D. #10 to a low of 2.9% in C.D. #16 (see Table 2.5). Similarly, in 1996, estimates of the concentrations of seniors in the 17 Regional Health Authorities (RHAs) in the province ranged from 14.6% in the East Central RHA to 2.2% in the Northern Lights RHA. (These percentages are calculated from data published in 1995 by Alberta Health.) Generally, the percentage of seniors tends to be highest in southern RHAs and lowest in northern RHAs.

In summary, with respect to the distribution of the senior population in Alberta, there are two notable dimensions. First, the rural-urban pattern indicates a high and increasing concentration of elders in Alberta's urban centers. Second, the north-south dimension indicates a high concentration of elders in the southern half of the province. While the north might well experience significant population growth in the future, nevertheless, it is expected in the decades to come that a relatively small percentage of Alberta's seniors will reside in the northern areas of the province, both because the total number of people living in the North will tend to be small relative to the total population living in the South, and because the population in the North tends to be relatively young, that is, has a low percentage of seniors. Of course, one cannot ignore those places where seniors are relatively few in number or make up a relatively small proportion of the population. Nevertheless, low numbers and low concentrations of seniors do increase the challenges of providing adequate services.

Alberta Census Divisions and Major Cities, 1991
Source: Statistics Canada 1991.

Map 2.1

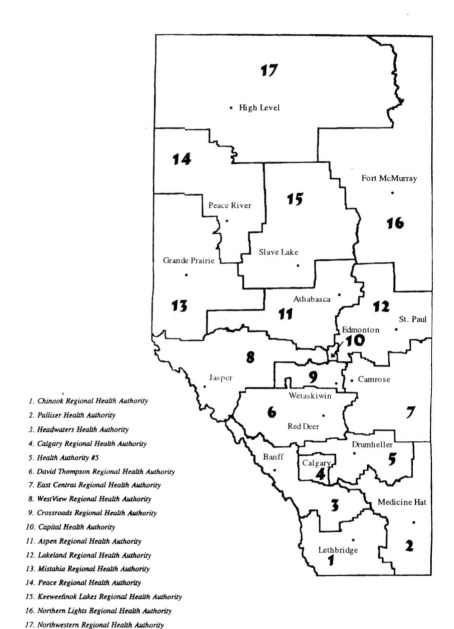

1. *Chinook Regional Health Authority*
2. *Palliser Health Authority*
3. *Headwaters Health Authority*
4. *Calgary Regional Health Authority*
5. *Health Authority #5*
6. *David Thompson Regional Health Authority*
7. *East Central Regional Health Authority*
8. *WestView Regional Health Authority*
9. *Crossroads Regional Health Authority*
10. *Capital Health Authority*
11. *Aspen Regional Health Authority*
12. *Lakeland Regional Health Authority*
13. *Mistahia Regional Health Authority*
14. *Peace Regional Health Authority*
15. *Keeweetinok Lakes Regional Health Authority*
16. *Northern Lights Regional Health Authority*
17. *Northwestern Regional Health Authority*

Regional Health Authorities, 1995

Map 2.2.

Age Structures and Life Expectancies

In 1996, the median age of Albertans was projected to be about 33 years (Statistics Canada, 1994a) meaning that half the population of Alberta was under 33 and half was over 33 years of age. By 2016, the median age is projected to rise to between 37 and 40 years of age, reflecting the aging of the baby boomers, declines in fertility, increases in life expectancy, and migration patterns (Statistics Canada, 1994a). Current trends in life expectancy are particularly interesting. For most of this century, life expectancy has been increasing for both men and women, although it has increased faster for women than for men, such that by the mid-1970s the difference in life expectancy for men and women was over 7 years (Statistics Canada, 1988:12). As women's life expectancy approaches its natural upper limits (i.e., the biologically determined female life span), the rate of increase in female life expectancy should slow. Furthermore, as men increasingly improve their lifestyles, their life expectancy should continue to increase and begin to catch up, in part at least, with women's life expectancy. It is not known what proportion of the gender difference in life expectancies is biologically based and what proportion reflects differences in lifestyles. Nevertheless, as male and female lifestyles converge, their life expectancies should also begin to converge (on the biologically based differential, whatever that is). Life expectancy data appear to show the beginning of this trend; indeed, from 1976 to 1991 the gender differential in life expectancy decreased from 7.1 years to 6.2 years in Alberta (Statistics Canada, 1994a:27-28). Statistics Canada assumes that by 2016 life expectancy will have increased for Alberta males from 75.0 years in 1991 to somewhere between 77.5 and 81.5 years and for Alberta females from 81.2 years to somewhere between 83.3 and 86.3 years. This is a closing of the gender differential for Albertans from 6.2 years in 1991 to somewhere between 4.8 and 5.8 years in 2016. This trend has interesting implications for future sex ratios, rates of widowhood for men and women, and so on. It is sometimes argued that aging is primarily a female problem, given that women tend to outlive men and therefore make up the majority of seniors, widowed persons, residents of institutions, and so on. While women will continue to predominate among the aged, as the gender difference in life expectancy declines, women will become somewhat less predominant in the senior population.

Note that life expectancy is an average. It tells you that, if the life expectancy for women is 80 years, one-half of women born today will die **before** their 80th birthday while the other half of these women will die **after** their 80th birthday. Consider also that life expectancy is a forecast, an attempt to divine the future. This forecast is based on the assumptions that the current (age-specific) pattern of deaths will not change during the lifetimes of these women. It follows then that if death rates go down, the life expectancy of women will be underestimated; if death rates should go up, their life expectancy would be overestimated.

There is another intriguing point to be made with respect to life expectancy. In 1991, in Alberta, males 65 years of age had a life expectancy of over 16 years. Consider that the resulting life expectancy of 81 (65 + 16) considerably exceeds the current life expectancy at birth of 75 years. Similarly, Alberta females, at 65 years of age in 1991, had a life expectancy of over 20 years. Even at the age of

85, half of males were expected to live longer than 5.9 years and half of females were expected to live longer than 7.3 years (Seniors Advisory Council for Alberta, 1993:13). The reason that life expectancy appears to increase with increasing age is that the original calculations include those who will die at younger ages as well as those who will survive to older ages. Later calculations are based on the survivors' chances; those who have died at younger ages and who therefore "brought down the average" being removed from the equation. Putting the statistical intricacies aside, the point is that very old people generally have far longer to live than one might assume.

Another way to look at age structure involves comparisons of different age groups using the so-called dependency ratios. One has to remember that population aging, which implies an increase in the ratio of seniors to the working age population, is primarily a function of declining fertility. Declines in fertility, however, imply a decrease in the ratio of children to the working age population. In short, the elderly dependency ratio is rising at the same time that the youth dependency ratio is falling (Seniors Advisory Council for Alberta, 1993:10; Alberta Bureau of Statistics, 1988:78). Too often, discussions of population aging focus only on the increase in the seniors' dependency ratio, and it is tempting to walk down the garden path and conclude that in the future the province will not be able to afford the support services promised its dependent populations. However, the important point is that the rise in the elderly dependency ratio is counterbalanced to some degree by the decline in the youth dependency ratio. A practical implication of these trends is that resources invested in young people during the past baby boom could be invested in services for seniors during the future seniors boom. If shifts in age structures are accompanied by shifts in the distribution of social resources, then the future costs of an increasingly aged population would be offset to a degree by the declining costs of a relatively diminishing population of young people. Nevertheless, any future reallocation of resources from the young to the old will depend more on politics than on demographics per se.

Sex Ratio

Slightly more males are born than females. However, because females currently live longer than males, in 1991, there were 130 elderly females in Alberta for every 100 elderly males. For persons over 85 years of age in Alberta the ratio was 185 older women for every 100 older men (Seniors Advisory Council for Alberta, 1993:5). This sex ratio had been increasing for some time, reflecting the divergence in male and female life expectancies. If, however, male and female life expectancies are now beginning to converge, then the seniors' sex ratios should also begin to converge. Indeed, Statistics Canada (1994a) population projections for Alberta show a sex ratio in 2016 of some 120 to 125 elderly women for every 100 elderly men, down from 130 in 1991.

Not only is the seniors' sex ratio changing in Alberta, but there are also substantial variations around the province. Table 2.9 shows that, in 1991, Alberta's cities tended to have more older women than older men (Red Deer was highest with 149 women 65+ years of age for every 100 men aged 65 and older). Census Divisions (CDs) in the southern half of the province also tended to have high seniors' sex ratios (CD #6 including the City of Calgary was highest at 141). However, CDs in the northern half of the province tended to have relatively lower seniors' sex ratios. Indeed, CDs 16, 17, and 18, which are located in Northern Alberta, had more older men than older woman (seniors' sex ratios of 98, 91, and 74 women 65+ years of age for every 100 men aged 65 and older). Similarly, for persons aged 75 years and older, sex ratios ranged from a high in Calgary of 182 women aged 75+ years of age for every 100 men aged 75+ years to a low of 86 in CD #18. While there are more elderly women than elderly men in Alberta as a whole, one cannot assume that this is true of every part of the province.

Marital Status

Women are more likely than men to be widowed because women live longer than men, and also because women typically marry older men. Furthermore, if widowed, men are more likely to remarry (Northcott, 1984). For these reasons, in 1991 in Alberta about 3 in 4 elderly men were married in comparison to less than 2 in 4 elderly women. Of those Albertans over the age of 75, half of the elderly men but less than 1 in 10 elderly women were married. Relatively small percentages of either sex were either currently divorced, separated, or never married (Seniors Advisory Council for Alberta, 1993:14-15). In short, while the risk of losing one's spouse increases with increasing age, that risk is far greater for women. Given that the presence of a spouse is a major source of social and economic support, older women are not only likely to find themselves without a spouse but also are more likely to become poor, institutionalized, and so on. A man has a fairly good chance of having a spouse in his old age. A woman does not have that guarantee.

If the life expectancy of men and women does indeed converge in the future, then the discrepancy in the risk of widowhood will also converge to a degree. Women will continue to be at greater risk, however, unless they start marrying younger men.

Given rising divorce rates, it might be anticipated that in the future larger proportions of seniors will be divorced. However, divorce is most common early in a marriage and is often followed by remarriage. It will therefore be true that more seniors in the future will have been divorced at some time in their life, but it is not necessarily true that there will be significant proportions of seniors who will be currently divorced. While the proportion of divorced seniors is likely to rise, it is also likely to remain relatively small.

Table 2.9
Sex Ratios (Number of Elderly Females per 100 Elderly Males)
for Census Divisions and Major Cities in Alberta, 1991

Census Divisions (and Major Cities)	Sex Ratio for Persons 65+ Years of Age	Sex Ratio for Persons 75+ Years of Age
1	129	144
(Medicine Hat)	(134)	(149)
2	133	148
(Lethbridge)	(145)	(160)
3	124	124
4	104	127
5	122	141
6	141	176
(Calgary)	(144)	(182)
7	115	127
8	126	141
(Red Deer)	(149)	(171)
9	107	115
10	120	129
11	136	164
(Edmonton)	(142)	(172)
12	107	117
13	101	116
14	109	126
15	124	140
16	98	95
(Fort McMurray)	(138)	(150)
17	91	96
18	74	86
19	114	126
(Grande Prairie)	(139)	(153)
Alberta	130	152

Source: Adapted from Statistics Canada. 1991 Census of Canada.
Catalogue Number 95-372.

The proportion of the population that never marries is generally quite small (under 10%) and somewhat higher for males than for females (Seniors Advisory Council for Alberta, 1993:15). The implications of never marrying (and also of being married, divorced, widowed, or remarried) for social support in old age are explored in some detail by Connidis (1989). Generally speaking, while a spouse is an important family tie for many seniors, those without a spouse typically benefit from a variety of other family ties. Despite the stereotypes, being never married or widowed does not necessarily imply being "alone" without family supports or social connections. Nevertheless, seniors who are widowed, divorced, or never married are more likely to be poor and are more likely to be institutionalized.

Living Arrangements

The great majority of seniors live in their own homes. The likelihood of renting accommodations increases with increasing age as does the likelihood of institutionalization. Women are more likely than men to rent or to be institutionalized, in part because they are more likely to be widowed. Nevertheless, virtually all seniors 65-74 years of age in Alberta live in private households, as do the great majority of seniors 75 years of age and older. While the risk of institutionalization increases with increasing age, in 1991, only 2.8% of Albertans 65-74 years of age and 18.3 % of Albertans 75 or more years of age resided in collective dwellings such as lodges, nursing homes, hospitals, rooming houses, and so on (Seniors Advisory Council for Alberta, 1993:16-17).

Of great significance, I think, is the trend in institutionalization evident in census data that show that in 1976, 13.4% of seniors in Alberta resided in collective dwellings (primarily lodges, nursing homes, and hospitals). In 1981 this figure dropped to 12.8% and in 1986 dropped again to 10.2%. By 1991, 9.0% of Alberta's seniors lived in collective dwellings (Seniors Advisory Council for Alberta, 1993:20). These declines might signify the success of Alberta's home care program (begun in 1978), seniors' apartments, and various other strategies designed to support seniors in their own homes. Alternatively, this trend might reflect the increased desire and/or ability of seniors to maintain their own independence. Seniors may be both healthier and wealthier than in the past (Engelmann, 1987:11-12) and therefore better able to preserve their independence. Conversely, a shortage of institutional beds might also produce such a trend, but this has not generally been the case for Alberta. This trend towards lower rates of institutionalization is true for both the 65-74 year olds and the 75+ year olds.

Socio-Economic Status

Socio-economic status is usually measured in terms of education, employment (occupation), and income or wealth. In terms of education, younger cohorts tend to have more years of formal schooling than older cohorts (Seniors Advisory Council for Alberta, 1993:23), suggesting that each successive "generation" of seniors will be better educated. Given that higher education tends to be associated with higher incomes and better health, this trend towards better educated seniors may imply a trend towards healthier and wealthier seniors (Engelmann, 1987:12). Of course, there is no guarantee that an association observed today between educational status and health status will necessarily continue to be observed in the future. As the population in general becomes more widely educated, this relationship might moderate or disappear. Further, while poverty has generally been the greater threat to health, there are "diseases of affluence." These caveats notwithstanding, it seems likely that seniors in the future will enjoy a trend towards better education and higher standards of living and health.

In 1991, 20% of elderly male and 8% of elderly female Albertans (excluding seniors residing in lodges, nursing homes, and so on) reported that they were in the labor force (Seniors Advisory Council for Alberta, 1993:24). Self-employed farmers, businesspersons, and professionals, for example, do not face mandatory retirement and often remain active in the labor force past the age of 65. Nevertheless, the trend has been towards decreased participation of senior males and the participation rates of senior females have remained low (McDonald and Wanner, 1990; for a discussion of the older worker, see Tindale, 1991). While the possible dismantlement of mandatory retirement could in the future bring about the increased involvement of seniors in paid employment, it seems more likely that the labor force participation rates of seniors will continue to decline (McDonald and Wanner, 1990).

Income and wealth are two different things. Wealth refers to a person's accumulated assets. Income usually refers to the money earned through employment or investments as reported to Revenue Canada in the preceding year. While income and wealth are often associated, a person may be wealthy and report little or no income, or may have little wealth and yet report a substantial income. An elderly farmer might own the farm, the house, the outbuildings, and the machinery and yet have so little income as to be classified as "poor" (i.e., having an income falling below the Statistics Canada low income cut-off point, the so-called poverty line). Cash poor, but assets rich! Generally speaking, the major asset of seniors is typically their home and seniors are more likely to own their home and to have little or no mortgage. However, the homes seniors own tend to be older, to be more in need of repair, and to have relatively lower resale value (National Council of Welfare, 1984a:57-60). In discussing poverty in old age it is important to remember that the usual discussion focuses on income (i.e., last year's reported income) and ignores wealth.[6]

Turning now to income, generally speaking the income of seniors in Canada and in Alberta in particular has been rising. Accordingly, the poverty rate for seniors has been declining (National Council of Welfare, 1996a:12-19, 85). These improvements in elderly incomes reflect both public- and private-sector trends. With respect to public sources of income, virtually all elderly Albertans receive the federal Old Age Security (OAS) payment monthly (and adjusted quarterly, i.e., indexed, to protect against inflation), although, since 1989, wealthier seniors have had to "pay back" some or all of their OAS payments when filing their annual income tax returns (Novak, 1993:232). Low income older Albertans also receive income supplements from the federal government (the guaranteed income supplement – GIS) and from the provincial government (the Alberta Seniors Benefit). Further, low income near-elderly spouses (ages 60-64) of senior citizens receive the federal spouse's allowance. Near-elderly low income widowed persons may receive the federal widowed spouse's allowance (for persons 60-64 years of age) or the Alberta widows' pension (for persons 55-64 years of age). All of these programs are income-tested, i.e., directed to lower-income seniors, except Old Age Security which excludes only the wealthiest seniors. Furthermore, increasing proportions of seniors have established their eligibility for Canada Pension Plan benefits. In short, there has been a significant increase in both the number of income support programs and in the level of benefits available to seniors.

Nevertheless, only about one-half of the income of seniors comes from public sources (National Council of Welfare, 1984a:42), and this dependency on public funds may be decreasing. In Alberta, the percentage of seniors receiving the maximum guaranteed income supplement (the federal GIS) has been declining (Seniors Advisory Council for Alberta, 1993:44-45). This trend suggests that seniors are increasingly enjoying income from such sources as the Canada Pension Plan, private pensions, personal savings and investment income (encouraged in part by the federal government's registered retirement savings plan), employment income, and so on.

While the income of seniors generally has been improving, problems remain. Income and wealth are not distributed evenly among seniors. First of all, in 1992 in Alberta, 5.6% of seniors received the maximum GIS, meaning that they had little or no other income than the OAS. Another 33.9% of seniors received partial GIS meaning that they had modest incomes from other sources than the OAS. Over half of seniors in Alberta (60.5%) had sufficient income that they did not require any supplementation (Seniors Advisory Council for Alberta, 1993:44-45). Of these, some were "near poor" while others were more well-to-do. Second, the risk of being (income) poor increases with increasing age, and is higher for women and for persons without a spouse (Seniors Advisory Council for Alberta, 1993:46-47; National Council of Welfare, 1996a). Third, there are substantial regional differences in the province with seniors in the northern region being most disadvantaged economically. While 15% of seniors in the northern region received the full GIS in 1992, only 4% of seniors residing in Calgary and 5% of seniors in Edmonton received the full guaranteed income supplement. Furthermore, 4% of seniors in the southern region and 7% of seniors in the central region received the maximum GIS (Seniors Advisory Council for Alberta, 1993:47-48).

Aboriginal Seniors

In Alberta, there are 8 different Native languages spoken, 41 Indian Bands, 60 Reserves, and 8 Metis Settlements (Hohn, 1986a). According to the 1991 Census, there were 148 220 persons in Alberta (5.8% of the population) who identified themselves as having at least one Aboriginal ancestor (Aboriginal Health Unit, Alberta Health, no date; Statistics Canada, 1995a:178). Of these, 23 785 lived on a Reserve, including 865 seniors (3.6% of the total population living on Reserves). The 1991 Census indicated that 2.3% of non-institutionalized Aboriginal persons in Alberta (3435 persons) were 65 years of age or older compared to 8.3% of the total non-institutionalized Alberta population, reflecting the Native population's higher birth rate and lower life expectancy. The great majority of older Natives live on the Reserve or in rural areas; very few live in the larger cities in Alberta (Hohn, 1986a; see also Seniors Advisory Council for Alberta, 1990).

The Labor Force

There is one final demographic feature of the "aging" population to which I would like to draw attention. A great deal of emphasis is placed on the increasing proportion of the population that is elderly, and concern is frequently expressed that this segment of the population will become literally too taxing a burden for some future labor force. This concern sometimes seems to be based on the assumptions that seniors are very expensive to support and that if there are more seniors then there will be fewer people available to support them. That is, there will be relatively fewer people in the labor force supporting an increasingly large and increasingly costly senior population. Denton, et al. (1986) note that this scenario emphasizes the changes in "demand" for support but largely ignores the "supply" side of the equation. That is, we also need to examine the trends affecting the size and productivity of the labor force.

First of all, while it is expected that there will be proportionately more seniors in the future, there are likely to be relatively fewer children, and the population of working age may well remain relatively constant (Alberta Bureau of Statistics, 1988:8; see also Statistics Canada, 1994a:80). Furthermore, the actual labor force may well grow as more and more women seek employment and might also grow if seniors continue in their employment should mandatory retirement be dismantled and present preferences for voluntary and early retirement decline. The ability of the labor force to support the senior population will also depend on the extent of unemployment and underemployment in the future. If high proportions of the labor force are, first of all, employed, and, second of all, engaged in full time "careers," tax revenues will be substantial. High rates of unemployment or of underemployment (part-time or seasonal work or pay at or near the minimum wage) will lower the labor force's ability to support its dependent populations. Finally, labor force technology (consider robotics) may well make the labor force more productive. In summary, while a great deal of effort is focused on forecasting the size of the future elderly population and estimating seniors' future needs, too little effort is invested in forecasting the size, composition, and productivity of the future labor force. Discussions about future costs have to encompass both estimates of future need and estimates of future ability to pay. In other words, we need to study labor force trends as well as the aging of the population.

Summary

Population aging, driven primarily by declining birth rates, has resulted in wide discrepancies in the percentage of seniors in various countries worldwide. In Canada, declining fertility, declining mortality, and migration have resulted in substantial variations in the percentage aged between provinces in Canada and within Alberta. Projections based on assumptions regarding fertility, mortality, and migration show that Alberta's aging trend is likely to continue well into the next century. There is evidence that the gender differential in mortality has peaked and is beginning to converge as male life expectancy begins to gain on female life expectancy. Should this trend continue, the sex ratio and the ratio of widows to widowers should also begin to converge. Other notable trends in Alberta include a declining rate of institutionalization for seniors and a declining rate of dependency on the federal guaranteed income supplement. Finally, while demographic aging suggests increased costs in the future, ability to pay is also influenced by the productivity and relative size of the labor force. It is important to pay attention not only to aging trends but also to labor force trends.

Chapter Three
The Social Epidemiology of Aging

Epidemiology studies the origins and distribution of disease in a population in hopes of identifying ways to control disease. Health, illness, disability, and death in human populations are not purely biological phenomena, and have many socio-cultural causes, consequences, and correlates. For example, health reflects lifestyles, living conditions, working conditions, socio-economic status (income, occupation, education), marital status, and family relationships. Even variables such as age and sex imply more than simple biology. Sex, for example, is associated with the likelihood of being or having been a smoker and with the risk of widowhood and poverty. Similarly, age also implies a history of social experiences and conditions. A person who was 65 years of age in 1995 and who was therefore born in 1930 will have had a different history than a person who will be 65 years of age in 2020, having been born in 1955. The person born in 1930 has experienced the economic depression of the 1930s, the Second World War, and the diet, lifestyle, and living conditions typical of those periods of time. The second person, born a quarter of a century later, has a different history, a different pattern of stresses and strains, advantages and disadvantages. These differences, accumulated over a lifetime, may well lead to both differential patterns of health and illness and to differential expectations for health care. The purpose of this chapter is to examine major trends in health, illness, disability, and death and explore several possible future scenarios. In this chapter I will also review and analyze various surveys of the "needs" of seniors in Alberta.

Changing Patterns of Mortality

The demographic transition was described in the preceding chapter. You will recall that the demographic transition is initiated by a decline in death rates. This transformation in patterns of dying is known as the epidemiologic transition (Omran, 1971). Olshansky and Ault (1986) describe four historical stages. In the first stage – identified as the age of pestilence and famine – infectious diseases are rampant, infant mortality is high, and average life expectancy is low. During the second stage – the age of receding pandemics – infectious diseases are increasingly brought under control. In this stage, death rates decline and average life expectancy increases. In the third stage – the age of degenerative and man-made diseases – death typically comes later in life as a result of degenerative diseases such as cancer, heart disease, or stroke. Infant mortality is low as are death rates from infectious diseases. Life expectancy is high. It is implied that patterns of death in stage three significantly reflect lifestyle choices and man-made living conditions. Olshansky and Ault also describe a fourth stage which they call the age of delayed degenerative diseases. As life expectancy continues to rise, the timing of death increasingly approaches the biological upper limit for our species. People continue to die of degenerative diseases; however, these deaths occur later and later in life. Stage four describes a scenario in which people typically live out their full and natural life span, dying in old age from senescent decline.

In Alberta today, the deadly epidemics of smallpox, cholera, polio, influenza, tuberculosis, and so on are largely behind us. Infant and maternal mortality are low; life expectancy is high. Death typically occurs late in life from heart disease, cancer, or stroke. Nevertheless, life expectancy continues to rise in Alberta, and the province, like many developed nations, has enjoyed recent dramatic declines in mortality from heart disease (for a brief discussion of this trend in Canada, see Statistics Canada, 1988:6, 8; see also Wilkins, 1996). In other words, Alberta would appear to be entering the fourth stage of the epidemiologic transition. Of course, progress is not inevitable and reversals are possible. AIDS is a case in point. Nevertheless, the epidemiologic transition describes a process which Alberta has already largely undergone. Hopefully, the victories won against disease and death will be enjoyed by Albertans for generations to come. Healthy lifestyle choices, healthy environments, and healthy public policies will go a long way toward ensuring a future with low rates of morbidity and mortality.

Changing Patterns of Morbidity

The discussion of the epidemiologic transition largely focuses on patterns of mortality (death). Of course, patterns of morbidity (sickness) have also changed. Not only are people less likely to die early in life from infectious diseases, but rising standards of living and practices such as immunization mean that young people are also less likely to get sick. Not only are people more likely to die in old age from chronic disease, but people are also more likely to live long enough to have chronic conditions and are more likely to survive with their chronic diseases. Just as people are increasingly living longer lives, so also people may be living in a healthy state for longer periods of their lives (McDaniel, 1986:82; Stone and Fletcher, 1986).

However, even if people are living longer and are healthier longer, does this mean that they are sick for shorter periods of their lives? Not necessarily! If we assume that life expectancy will increase in the future and also that there will be a delay in the onset of morbidity (i.e., people will be healthier longer), then there are three possibilities regarding the future extent of the average duration of ill health. Figure 3.1 diagrams the average life expectancy and indicates the average age at onset of health problems that lead ultimately to the death of the individual. Now, it is in fact often difficult to identify the "onset of morbidity" and I will leave the operationalization of that concept to others. For the purposes of my discussion I will assume that the onset of morbidity is easily identified. Figure 3.1 shows that the present average duration of morbidity leading to death is X years. For example, cancer is diagnosed, or a heart attack or stroke occurs, culminating X years later in death. Figure 3.1 next illustrates three possible scenarios for the future, assuming in every case that life expectancy increases from its present level.

In the first future scenario, which might be called the expansion of morbidity model, death is delayed substantially; however, the onset of morbidity is delayed only a little. The result is that while people in the future live longer lives on average and are healthier longer, they are also sick for a longer period of time preceding their death. This scenario might materialize in the future if we are increasingly successful in improving survival rates for people with chronic disease, but are not significantly successful in "preventing" (i.e., forestalling) disease. Suppose, however, that health promotion and disease prevention are achieved to a greater degree. In future scenario two, which might be called the delay of morbidity model, the onset of morbidity is delayed to the same degree as the delay in death. In this scenario, people live longer and are healthier longer, but on average are sick for about the same amount of time preceding their death as they are now. Finally, in future scenario three, while death is delayed, the onset of morbidity is delayed even more resulting in a compression of the period of morbidity into a shorter and shorter period of time. This compression of morbidity model has received a great deal of attention (see, for example, Fries, 1980 and 1983).

Present	a	b	X	c
Future 1	a		b	c
Future 2	a		b	c
Future 3	a		b	c

where a=birth, b=onset of morbidity leading to death, c=death, a→c=life expectancy, and b→c=average duration of morbidity preceeding death, presently X years.

Figure 3.1 Three Future Scenarios Regarding the Onset of Morbidity and the Average Duration of Morbidity Preceeding Death.

If there is a compression of morbidity in Alberta in the future, then the costs of caring for an aging Alberta population will not be as great as current patterns of morbidity suggest (see, for example, Hertzman and Hayes, 1985). On the other hand, compression of morbidity may be overly optimistic (see, for example, Barer, et al., 1995:219; Roos, et al., 1993; Verbrugge, 1989 and 1984; Evans, 1989; Bury, 1988; Kraus, 1988; Simmons-Tropea and Osborn, 1987; Feldman, 1983; Schneider and Brody, 1983) and the extent of morbidity may remain more-or-less as it is today, or may even increase.

Expansions in the average length of morbidity imply increases in the cost of care only if similar care is provided. In other words, if one is ultimately concerned with the costs of caring for an aging population, then one must examine not only trends in morbidity, one must also examine trends in service delivery and in the "demand" for services (see, for example, Barer, et al., 1995; Black, et al., 1995;

Culyer, 1988:30-33; Barer, et al., 1987 and 1986; Evans, 1987a and 1987b; Roos, Shapiro, and Roos, 1987:338-342). Trends in service delivery will be discussed later in chapter five. In the remainder of this chapter, I will review and analyze studies and surveys of seniors in Alberta in an effort to identify their needs and expectations for services. The following discussion will go beyond a narrow focus on medical problems and medical services and I will examine a broad range of issues that have a bearing on the "physical, mental and social well-being" (1946 Constitution of the World Health Organization; Mechanic, 1978:53; Antonovsky, 1980:52) of seniors. I will first review the utilization of health care services by elderly Albertans and then review surveys of Alberta's seniors.

Utilization of Health Care Services by Elderly Albertans

In 1991, seniors made up 8.6% of the Alberta population. In 1991-92, seniors in Alberta used 20.2% of physical therapy services, 50.2% of podiatry care, 9.7% of chiropractic care, 11.1% of optometry services, 42.7% of patient days in general hospitals, and were 22.5% of patients discharged. Average length of stay in the general hospital was 13 days for seniors compared to 5 days for non-seniors. While seniors in 1993 made up 9.7% of persons served by community mental health clinics and in 1992 received about 7% of community health nurses' direct service time, seniors in 1991-92 constituted 86% of clients served by the Home Care Program. In 1993, 50.5% of persons who had been declared legally dependent (under the Dependent Adults Act) were seniors, many of these residing in institutions. In 1992, 91.5% of residents in long term care centres (formerly called nursing homes and auxiliary hospitals and increasingly being referred to as continuing care centres) were seniors (44.2% were 85 years of age or older). An increasing proportion of residents in long term care require "heavy" as opposed to "light" care. (See Seniors Advisory Council for Alberta, 1993:61-100). In 1994/95 males 65 to 74 years of age used physicians' services over twice as much as the average male Albertan, while males 75 and older used almost three times the average level of service. Similarly, in 1994/95 females 65 to 74 years of age used physicians' services about one and a half times as much as the average female Albertan, while females 75 and older used almost two times the average level of service.[1]

While it is well-known that seniors are at higher risk than non-seniors for health problems and consume a disproportionate amount of health care and institutional services, these data tend to reinforce the stereotype that all seniors are sick, dependent, institutionalized, and so on. This is not true. At any one time, the majority of seniors report that their health is good to excellent (Alberta Senior Citizens Secretariat, 1989a:5; see also Roos, Shapiro, and Roos, 1987) and the great majority of seniors continue to live independently. Note that in 1991, only 2.8% of Albertans 65-74 years of age lived in "collective dwellings" (mostly lodges, nursing homes, and hospitals) as did 18.3% of those 75 years of age and older – still a significant minority. Overall, only 9.0% of Alberta's seniors lived in institutions in 1991 (Seniors Advisory Council for Alberta, 1993:16-17).

The rates of institutionalization for Alberta's seniors appear to be trending downwards (from 13.4% in 1976 to 9.0% in 1991 for seniors of all ages; for the 65-74 year olds, from 6.7% in 1976 to 2.9% in 1991; and for the 75+ year olds, from 24.4% in 1976 to 18.7% in 1991) (Seniors Advisory Council for Alberta, 1993:20), reflecting increases in health and wealth (factors fostering independence) and the effects of such programs as home care, which are designed to prevent or forestall institutionalization. Nevertheless, the increases in the number of senior citizens in the future will mean a continuing need for institutional services in the province. In other words, the aging of the population implies increased costs while the declines in the rates of institutionalization imply decreased costs, with these two trends counterbalancing each other to some degree.

While the rates of institutionalization of seniors have been trending downward, the rates of utilization of medical (doctor) services have been rising for some time now for both seniors and non-seniors alike in Alberta. Indeed, while seniors tend to use almost two times as many services per capita as the general population, nevertheless, the **rate of increase** in usage has been greater for the general population than for seniors (Seniors Advisory Council for Alberta, 1993:63-66). Rising utilization rates coupled with population aging trends imply substantial cost increases in the future. The factors influencing the usage of medical services will be discussed further in chapter five.

While the majority of seniors at any one time are reasonably healthy and live independently, nevertheless, when health problems strike, they are often more serious or longer lasting than for non-seniors. For example, while only a small percentage of seniors are hospitalized in a given year, average length of stay is almost three times as long as non-seniors. Furthermore, risk is associated with age, sex, socio-economic status, and marital and family status. Generally, health care utilization and/or institutionalization increases with increasing age, is higher for persons lacking economic resources and/or family supports, and is higher for women (who are more likely than men to be older, widowed, and poor) (Alberta Senior Citizens Secretariat, 1989b:51-76).

Surveys of Seniors in Provinces Other Than Alberta

An exhaustive review of the various surveys of seniors conducted in each of Canada's provinces and territories is beyond the scope of this study. The interested reader might wish to consult existing annotated bibliographies which review research on aging conducted, for example, in Manitoba (see Rempel, 1987; Manitoba Association on Gerontology, 1983), Saskatchewan (see Saskatchewan Senior Citizens' Provincial Council, 1983), and British Columbia (see Simon Fraser University Gerontology Research Centre, 1989 and 1984). Some of the more extensive and better known provincial and local studies of seniors are reviewed in the following (national studies are discussed separately).

Manitoba's program of aging research has been quite extensive. The first of the "Aging in Manitoba" surveys was conducted in 1971 (Manitoba Department of Health and Social Development, 1973; Havens, 1980). At that time, random samples of elderly Manitobans 65 years of age and older living in the community (n=3558) and living in institutional facilities (n=1247) were interviewed regarding their needs and resources available to meet those needs. In addition, 680 agencies providing services for seniors were surveyed. This study found that generally there were adequate resources to meet the needs of seniors but that these services needed to be more accessible.

In 1976, a shortened version of the 1971 questionnaire was administered to a sample of non-institutionalized elderly Manitobans 60 years of age and older (n=1302) and to resource agencies serving seniors' needs (Manitoba Department of Health and Community Services, n.d.; Hull, 1979). In 1983, a third survey of elderly Manitobans 60 years of age and older (n=2854) and resource agencies serving seniors was conducted (Manitoba Department of Health, 1987). In addition, the survivors of the 1971 and 1976 studies were re-interviewed (n=about 3200). A fourth survey was conducted in 1991 (Black, 1995:138).

The Manitoba Longitudinal Study on Aging (Mossey, et al., 1981) involved the merging of survey data (from the 1971 study) and health care utilization data from the Manitoba government's health care claims files for 1970 to 1977 (n=4709). This study found that

> . . . the elderly are not, as has often been assumed, high consumers of ambulatory physician visits and hospital days. Rather a small proportion of elderly account for a very large share of service use, and a person's utilization behaviors appear to remain consistent over time.

The data suggest also that: (1) the very old are at greater risk of hospitalization but use only marginally more ambulatory physician services than their younger counterparts; (2) while males are over represented in hospital use, females make slightly more visits to physicians; (3) the assessment of their health (self rated health and the number of self reported health problems) strongly predicts their subsequent health care use; (4) residents of senior citizen's housing units are at greater risk of using health care than other community residents; and (5) level of unmet need is related to subsequent use of health services. (Mossey, et al., 1981:557)

Roos, Montgomery, and Roos (1987) studied a representative sample of 60 000 Manitobans aged 45 and older including 4263 persons who died between July 1974 and June 1976. The sample was selected from the files of the provincial health insurance plan. Records of health care utilization in the four years preceding death were examined. It was found that health care utilization tends to be highest in the final year of life and tends to be higher for persons dying at the oldest ages. Similarly, Roos, et al. (1989) examined usage of hospitals and nursing homes over a 16-year period from 1970 to 1985 for over 4000 elderly Manitobans. In any given year, a small percentage of seniors used a high percentage of services. Further, while some persons do die "inexpensively," health care utilization and costs tend to be greatest for those persons who are dying. (For an analysis of the "high cost of dying" for American seniors, see Scitovsky, 1994.)

Prince Edward Island's seniors were surveyed in 1978-1980 (Prince Edward Island Department of Health and Social Services, 1981). Initially, a small number of case studies of seniors (both individuals and couples) were collected. In addition, most of the agencies delivering health and social services to seniors in the province were surveyed. Subsequently, 660 seniors living in the community, in senior citizens' housing, and in nursing homes were interviewed. This study found that most seniors either did not have serious unmet needs or they had sufficient informal resources to deal with their needs. In other words, the great majority of seniors were found to rely on informal resources for any needed help and very few relied on services provided by formal agencies (p. viii).

In 1981, two separate surveys of seniors were conducted in the province of Saskatchewan. The first study was a survey of 1267 seniors living in the community (Stolee, et al., 1982). This study found that the single greatest cause of dependency in the community was dementia, with a prevalence of about 1% for severe and about 3% for moderate dementia. The second study was a survey of 990 seniors living in 29 long-term care institutions (about 200 persons from each of the four levels of care) (Rockwood, et al., 1981). Institutionalized seniors were disproportionately female, widowed, and 85+ years of age. People were found not to "progress" through the levels of care – many were admitted at higher levels of care directly from the community following a stay in an acute-care hospital. The prevalence of dementia ranged from 21% in level I to 64+% in level IV patients. Fifteen percent of residents were thought to be capable of living in the community with very little support. The availability of social supports was an important factor determining whether dependent seniors were cared for at home or in an institution.

The Ontario Longitudinal Study of Aging followed an initial sample of 2000 males from 45 years of age in 1959 to 64 years of age in 1978 (while some died before the study was completed and others moved away or declined to participate further in the study, 1034 were still alive and participating in the study in 1978). This study was designed to examine the relationships among aging, socio-economic status, and health. Smoking was found to be the most significant determinant of mortality; furthermore, income was also found to be an important predictor (Hirdes and Forbes, 1989; see also Hirdes, et al., 1986).

The London, Ontario Community Study was conducted in 1981 (Connidis, 1987:457-468). This study involved interviews with 400 seniors living in the community. Forty of these respondents were interviewed further in order to obtain additional qualitative data. Connidis (1987) found that about 12% of seniors had used community services in the past, some 7% were using community services at the time they were interviewed, 4% needed services they either could not find or afford, and a total of 9% either relied on or needed community services. In other words, the great majority of seniors were not dependent on formal services. This implies that these seniors were either able to live independently or relied on informal supports such as family members. Nevertheless, Connidis (1983) found that seniors generally would prefer to move into an institution should they no longer be able to live alone rather than move in with their adult offspring.

Regarding seniors' overall view of old age, Connidis (1987:468) notes that:

... a much larger proportion of older individuals in this study like aspects
of being their age rather than dislike features of their age. A surprising
majority also report having no worries about growing older. This suggests
that older people tend to take a positive view of their stage of life. There
appear to be some unique elements of older age that are enjoyed by older
individuals: reduced responsibility, greater freedom, and maturity gained
from experience.

At the same time, large numbers of the sample document some negative
aspects of older age, most notably failing health, physical decline, and the
consequences of dependency and widowhood that often follow. This
indicates an awareness of the very real setbacks that may accompany older
age. In short, older people tend to combine a positive view of their stage
of life with a realistic grasp of its detriments.

The Hamilton and Stoney Creek, Ontario Study (Marshall, 1987b; Rosenthal,
1987) interviewed 468 persons in 1986. About a third of these respondents were
40-54 years of age, another third were 55-69, and the final third were 70 years
of age and older. In addition, questionnaires were mailed to the respondents'
children. This study found that while the likelihood of having a chronic condition
increased with age, most respondents said that they were able to do what they
wanted to do. Further, while the family was generally willing to care for aging
dependent parents, nevertheless, both parents and offspring tended to feel that
children were not "obligated" and that living together is often problematic. Just
the same, adult offspring tended to become more concerned about their parents
as they reached advanced old age, tended to monitor their needs, and were ready
to provide care, if necessary.

An exhaustive review of all of the findings and published results of these
various studies of seniors goes beyond the scope of this project. Further, many
other studies not reviewed here have been conducted in Canada. It is the purpose
of this monograph to focus primarily on Alberta and, therefore, I will conclude
this chapter with an extensive review of surveys of seniors done in that particular
province.

Surveys of Seniors in Alberta

National Surveys

There have been a number of national surveys of the general population that
have involved Albertans. These national surveys became increasingly common
in the 1980s and 1990s. A brief overview follows.

The Canadian Sickness Survey 1950-51 was Canada's first national health
survey (Department of National Health and Welfare and Dominion Bureau of
Statistics, 1960; see also Kohn, 1967). Some 10 000 households (including
persons of all ages) were surveyed. Generally, females, the elderly, and the poor
were more likely to be ill. Health care utilization (e.g., going to a doctor, being

admitted to a hospital) was higher for women and for the elderly. Nevertheless, on any given day, the majority of seniors reported good health.

The Nutrition Canada National Survey 1970-72 assessed the nutritional status of a sample of 19 000 Canadians of all ages (Nutrition Canada, 1973). Seniors were more likely to have poor dietary intakes of protein and vitamin A and were more likely to exhibit thiamin deficiency.

The Canada Health Survey 1978-79 sampled some 12 000 households (including persons of all ages) across Canada (Canada Health Survey, 1981). Seniors were less likely to be current drinkers of alcohol, to smoke tobacco currently, and to be physically active. Seniors were more likely to report health problems, days when confined to bed because of health problems (bed-disability), days when they could not perform their major activities because of health problems (major activity-loss days), total disability days (bed-disability days plus major activity-loss days plus days when they had to cut down because of health problems), hearing trouble, symptoms of anxiety and depression, taking medication, and taking multiple varieties of medication. Generally elderly females reported more health problems than older men, except for hearing problems where elderly males reported a higher rate of disability.

The Canada Fitness Survey 1981 studied a national sample of nearly 22 000 Canadians aged 10 and over who completed a questionnaire on their physical recreation patterns. Approximately 16 000 people under age 70 also did standardized fitness tests (Canada Fitness Survey, 1982). Cardiovascular fitness, flexibility, and muscular endurance were found to decline with increasing age. Women at all ages tended to be more flexible than men but had less muscular endurance. Physical activity was found to decline with increasing age. Seniors were more likely to say that their "doctor's advice" was a reason for being physically active. Seniors were also more likely to say that they did not wish to increase their present level of activity.

The Canadian Health and Disability Survey 1983-84 was the first national study focusing on long-term (six months or more) functionally limiting disabilities (e.g., vision, hearing, speech, and mobility) (Statistics Canada and Department of the Secretary of State of Canada, 1986). This study was done as a supplement to the monthly Labor Force Survey. Over 126 000 non-institutionalized people aged 15 and over (there was also a sample of children) were screened yielding about 16 000 persons with some form of disability. The latter were then interviewed about their limiting conditions. The likelihood of disability was found to increase sharply with age and almost 40% of Canadians aged 65+ were found to have some level of disability. (Over one-third of all disabled Canadians were seniors.) Problems with physical mobility/agility were reported most often by seniors, followed by hearing difficulties and then by uncorrected visual problems. Nevertheless, most seniors with disabilities reported that their level of impairment was moderate and most were able to take care of themselves independently. Seniors with disabilities were most likely to report that they were dependent on assistance with heavy household chores and yardwork. The causes of disability for seniors were most often diseases of the musculoskeletal system and connective tissue followed by diseases of the sense organs, particularly hearing disorders. Finally, disability rates for seniors appear to decline with increasing education, meaning that better-educated seniors have a lower risk of experiencing disability (or at least are less likely to report disability).

The Health Promotion Survey 1985 was the first national survey to examine health knowledge, attitudes, beliefs, and behaviors rather than health status per se (Health and Welfare Canada, 1987b). Over 11 000 persons were interviewed.[2] The General Social Survey 1985 also surveyed over 11 000 Canadians about health and lifestyle topics (Statistics Canada, 1987).[3] The data from these two national studies have been analyzed separately for Alberta.

The Alberta data from the 1985 General Social Survey (which focused on health, lifestyles, and on support available to seniors; n=1342 non-institutionalized Albertans aged 15+) have been analyzed by Parakulam and Odynak (1989). Similarly, the Alberta data from the 1985 Health Promotion Survey (n=2733 non-institutionalized Albertans 15+ years of age) have been analyzed by Parakulam (1987a). In addition, the Edmonton sample of the 1985 Health Promotion Survey was augmented (n=1754 non-institutionalized Edmontonians aged 15+) and analyzed by the Edmonton Board of Health (Macdonald and Kurji, 1986). In 1986, health risk factor surveys (based on the 1985 federal Health Promotion Survey) were carried out in the Peace River (n=508 persons aged 20+), Leduc-Strathcona (n=801), Sturgeon (n=789), and Minburn-Vermilion (n=455) Health Units (Parakulam 1987b; 1987c). While none of these studies focused on seniors exclusively, findings are often reported by age.

With respect to seniors in Alberta, the 1985 General Social Survey found that almost one-half of elderly male Albertans and over one-half of elderly female Albertans reported having arthritis/rheumatism, the most common of the chronic ailments (Parakulam and Odynak, 1989). Over one-third of senior Albertans reported hypertension (high blood pressure). The likelihood of having one or more chronic conditions increased with age and about 80% of elderly Albertans reported at least one chronic health problem.

The Health Promotion Survey 1985 found that older Albertans were less likely to smoke or drink alcohol (Parakulam, 1987a). The majority of Alberta seniors exercised frequently and most had had their blood pressure checked during the previous year. About one-in-five were overweight. Perceived health status declined with age and over one-third of Alberta seniors reported a long-term health problem which limited physical activity. Nevertheless, seniors were less likely than non-seniors to complain that their lives were stressful. The Edmonton sample of the Health Promotion Survey 1985 (augmented by the Edmonton Board of Health) produced similar findings (Macdonald and Kurji, 1986) as did the four Health Risk Factor Surveys carried out in four health units in 1986 (Parakulam 1987b; 1987c).

A second national Health Promotion Survey was conducted in 1990. This study updated and expanded the previous 1985 survey. Over 13 000 people were interviewed nationally, including an additional 1500 interviews in Alberta paid for by Alberta Health. A total of 2530 interviews were completed in Alberta (Health and Welfare Canada, 1993). The 1990 survey found that the majority of

Canadian seniors rated their health as very good or excellent compared to other persons of the same age. Furthermore, older adults perceived their lives to be less stressful than did younger adults (p. 248).

The General Social Survey, which began in 1985, has been conducted annually on a five-year cycle. That is, while the focus of the survey changes each year, a particular focus is revisited every five years. The 1985 focus on health, for example, was also the subject of the 1991 survey and is expected to be the focus again in 1996.

The 1986 General Social Survey, which focused on time use, found that seniors had more free time than non-seniors, were more likely to engage in leisure activities such as watching television, reading (books, magazines, newspapers), and participating in sports, hobbies, crafts, and cards or other games. Older people were more likely to spend time walking, slept longer, and spent more time on meals at home. Older people and younger people spent about the same amount of time on family care (Jones, 1990). The 1992 GSS, which again focused on time use, found that retirees spent more time on volunteer work (Devereaux, 1993).

The 1990 General Social Survey examined contacts with family and friends and assistance given and received. Together with the 1985 survey, which had also examined social support for seniors, these surveys found that older women tend to report a wider range of social supports and contacts than older men. While older men were more likely to rely on their spouse, they were less likely than older women to rely on a daughter or son, and more likely to not seek support from anyone. It was also found that the great majority of seniors reported they were happy and satisfied with the various aspects of their lives (Gauthier, 1991; McDaniel, 1993; McDaniel and McKinnon, 1993; Keith and Landry, 1992). The 1995 GSS was to focus again on social support (results were forthcoming at the time of writing).

The 1991 General Social Survey, like the 1985 survey, focused on health. The most common chronic condition, reported by over half of seniors, was arthritis/rheumatism. High blood pressure, heart trouble, high cholesterol, and allergies were also common. Nevertheless, most seniors indicated that they enjoyed good or very good health (Seniors Advisory Council for Alberta, 1993:36-38). The 1996 GSS will focus once again on health.

The Health and Activity Limitation Surveys of 1986-87 and 1991-92 (Statistics Canada, 1989 and 1994b) each consisted of three phases: 1. a two-part question on the census long form for 1986 and again in 1991 (filled out by one in every five households), 2. post-censal surveys of well over 100 000 non-institutionalized Canadians (of all ages) in 1986 and again in 1991, and 3. post-censal surveys of some 20 000 institutionalized Canadians (of all ages) in 1987 and another 10 000 in 1992. The 1986-87 study found that nearly half of Canadian seniors 65+ years of age and 82% of persons 85+ years of age had some form of disability. Nevertheless, the majority of seniors with disabilities were able to live relatively normal lives, although some were severely disabled and some were institutionalized (Nessner, 1990; Dunn, 1991; Dunn, 1990). The

1991-92 study again found that nearly half of Canadian seniors reported some form of disability (Statistics Canada, 1994b). The 1986-87 study estimated that about 90 000 elderly Albertans were disabled to some degree at least (e.g., impaired mobility, hearing, or vision). These disabled seniors made up about one-third of all of the disabled persons in the province (Statistics Canada, 1989; Alberta Health, Health Economics, and Statistics, 1991).

The 1988 Campbell's Survey on Well-Being in Canada (named for the Campbell's Soup Company who helped sponsor this research; see Stephens and Craig, 1990) involved a follow-up study conducted in 1988 of 4000 individuals who had participated in the 1981 Canada Fitness Survey. This study found that Canadians in general, and middle-aged and older Canadians in particular, increased their levels of physical activity from 1981 to 1988. While activity levels tended to decline with increasing age, nevertheless, according to some definitions, seniors were more active than middle-aged Canadians. Middle-aged and older Canadians were also found to be more likely than other age groups to limit their dietary consumption of fat, and were more likely to have reduced their consumption of red meat and total calories from 1981 to 1988. Seniors were more likely than non-seniors to eat three regular meals daily. While seniors were more likely than non-seniors to have utilized health care services (physician, hospital) recently, nevertheless, seniors were less likely to report having to restrict their daily routine for health reasons, were more likely to report positive emotional well-being, and (except for young adolescents) were more likely to rate their health as "very good."

The National Alcohol and Other Drugs Survey 1989 interviewed almost 12 000 Canadians 15+ years of age, excluding residents of institutions. Seniors were more likely to use prescription drugs than non-seniors. The most common prescriptions used by seniors were for the heart or for blood pressure. Twenty-seven percent of older women and 19% of older men reported using three or more prescription and/or non-prescription drugs in the previous month (Bergob, 1994).

The National Survey on Abuse of the Elderly in Canada 1989 (Podnieks, 1990) interviewed 2008 seniors living in private households. This survey found that 2.5% of seniors had experienced material abuse (financial exploitation) at some time since turning age 65, 1.4% had suffered chronic verbal aggression in the previous year, 0.5% (1 in every 200) had been physically abused at some time since turning age 65, and 0.4% reported being neglected in the past year. A total of 4 in every 100 seniors reported some form of mistreatment, with 19% of mistreated seniors reporting more than one form of abuse.

The Survey on Ageing and Independence 1991 (Government of Canada, 1993) interviewed some 20 000 persons, half of them 45-64 years of age ('tomorrow's seniors') and the other half 65+ year of age ('today's seniors'). Residents of institutions were excluded. This study examined a range of factors which contribute to the quality of life and independence of older persons, in particular, physical and mental well-being, social interaction, and income. This survey found that social support was exchanged mainly among family members and that persons aged 45 and older were more likely to give assistance than to receive it. It was also found that the great majority of both men and women 45 years of age and older reported that their current income met their needs either adequately or very well. Furthermore, two-thirds of persons 45-64 years of age felt that their future income would meet their needs as did even higher percentages of older persons (Elliot, et al., 1996:119, 121). Schellenberg (1994) has examined the "transition into retirement," drawing heavily on data from the 1991 Survey on Ageing and Independence.

The data for Alberta from the 1991 Survey on Ageing and Independence have been reported by Sefton and Mummery (1995). They note that almost all Albertans 45 years of age and older were satisfied with their economic security and that this satisfaction appeared to be higher for older respondents. They report that the main strategies used by people to prepare for their retirement were paying off or avoiding debts, building registered retirement savings plans (RRSPs), and building up other savings. While one-in-four persons 45 years of age and older suffered from some sort of limitation in activity because of a long term health problem(s), almost all said they were coping very well or fairly well with the problem. In regards to stress, widows were more likely than other marital status groups to report that their lives were not stressful at all. Eighty percent of respondents in Alberta said that they provided assistance to others, most often emotional support, transportation, housework, yardwork, meal preparation, and grocery shopping, in that order. Somewhat less than two-thirds of respondents in Alberta said that they received assistance, most often emotional support, yardwork, housework, grocery shopping, and transportation services, in that order.

The Canadian Study of Health and Aging 1991-92 examined the prevalence of dementia for seniors 65+ years of age in Canada. Representative samples of seniors in the community (n=9008) and in institutions (n=1255) were studied. It was found that 8% of seniors had dementia, with prevalence ranging from 2.4% of persons 65-74 years of age to 11.1% of persons 75-84 years of age to 34.5% of persons aged 85 and older. About 5% of seniors appeared to be suffering from Alzheimer's disease while 1.5% were diagnosed with vascular dementia (Canadian Study of Health and Aging Working Group, 1994).

In addition, The Canadian Study of Health and Aging conducted interviews with the caregivers of those persons diagnosed with dementia and with a comparison group of caregivers for non-demented persons (Canadian Study of Health and Aging, 1994). It was found that about half of all persons with dementia in Canada live in the community and virtually all have a caregiver. The caregiver is usually an unpaid family member, relative or friend, typically a spouse or daughter.

Among those caring for someone in the community, those caring for a person with dementia are more likely to experience chronic health problems and depressive symptoms than are those caring for a non-demented elderly person. Those caring for a person in the community are much more likely to feel burdened than those whose loved one is in an institution . . . The findings suggest that long-term care institutions are serving a role for Canada's seniors, particularly for the most demented, and that caregivers often provide care for loved ones even when suffering from chronic health conditions, depression, and burden themselves. (p. 471)

The National Population Health Survey of 1994-95 is scheduled to interview the same respondents every two years for up to two decades. This will be Canada's first national longitudinal health survey. Over 26 000 persons living in the community or in institutions were interviewed for the 1994-95 survey (Statistics Canada, 1995b). It was found that 36% of persons aged 75 or older rated their health as excellent or very good. While seniors 65 and older were less likely than other age groups to have suffered an injury in the past year, they were most likely (39% of seniors) to have a long-term activity limitation, usually as a consequence of chronic health conditions. At the time of writing, the data from the NPHS 1994-95 had only recently been released. The NPHS is a rich data set and will be the basis for many future analyses.

Provincial Surveys

While a number of surveys of seniors have been conducted in local areas of Alberta, there have been few province-wide seniors surveys originating within Alberta. Given the increasing prevalence of national surveys from which Alberta data can be extracted, there is perhaps little need at present for made-in-Alberta provincial surveys of seniors.

Turning to specific studies of Alberta seniors, in 1976, a sample of 1089 Albertans (one-half were retired and the other half were over 45 years of age and working) were surveyed to determine those factors which led to satisfaction or dissatisfaction in retirement (Third Career Research Society, 1976). "Freedom," social contacts, and hobbies and activities were found to be important sources of satisfaction, while poor health and inadequate income were major sources of dissatisfaction for those so disadvantaged.

In 1986, 1124 residents of senior citizen lodges throughout Alberta were surveyed (Alberta Municipal Affairs, 1987). Most lodge residents were over 75 years of age (average 81.3 years), female (60%), and not currently married (85%). Average age at admission was 78 years and reasons for admission centered on the difficulties of living alone (e.g., minor health problems, home maintenance, loneliness). About one-quarter of residents remain in the lodge until death, while the majority of those who leave for other reasons do so because they require higher levels of care. Residents were generally satisfied with the lodges.

The 1990 Senior Citizens' Lodge Survey (Alberta Health Facilities Review Committee, 1991) determined that the average age of residents in Alberta's 139 lodges was increasing. Over 86% of residents were 75 years of age or older and over 41% were 85 years of age or older. Two out of every three residents were female. Finally, lodge residents increasingly required health care services that exceeded the mandate of the lodges.

In 1988, the Alberta Resident Classification System for Long Term Care Facilities was initiated (Charles and Schalm, 1992a). This mechanism provides an annual classification of the nursing care requirements of the residents of

Alberta's long term care facilities (formerly nursing homes and auxiliary hospitals). The 1990 classification (Long Term Care Branch, Alberta Health, 1991; see Charles and Schalm, 1992b for 1988 classification data) reports that about 5% of Alberta's seniors were residents in long term care facilities. Furthermore, while not all residents were seniors, 91% were age 65 or older (78% were age 75 or older), the average age was 81 years, 66% were female, 76% were widowed/divorced/separated or never married, 25% required the lowest levels of care (levels A and B), 36% required the highest levels of care (levels F and G), 53% were identified as frail elderly residents and another 40% of residents (including some non-seniors) were cognitively impaired. The frail elderly tended to require lower levels of care on average than the cognitively impaired who tended to require higher levels of care. Sixty-one percent of residents received assistance from family members more than once a week. Less than 6% of residents did not receive any assistance from family members.

Ross, et al. (1995) studied adult day programs in rural and urban locations around Alberta, in the early 1990s. They interviewed 91 elderly clients of day support programs and 56 elderly clients of day hospital programs twice before entry to the program (2 months before entry and just before entry) and three times post-entry (at 2 weeks, 2 months, and 6 months post-entry). Average attendance was about 2 days per week. Ross, et al. found that half of the clients were 75 years of age or older, a third were cognitively impaired, a quarter suffered urinary incontinence, and a tenth suffered bowel incontinence. Most clients were in relatively close contact with other family members and reported a number of persons with whom they could talk or confide. Most of the people in the clients' social networks were perceived to be helpful and supportive most of the time. Clients rated their quality of life midway on a scale from worst to best possible quality of life. Clients rated their health, on average, as fair on a scale of excellent, very good, good, fair, and poor.

Ross, et al. (1995) also studied 122 informal caregivers of adult day program clients. These caregivers were typically the senior's spouse or daughter. One in four of the caregivers were 75 years of age or older. Older caregivers often had their own health problems while younger caregivers usually had multiple roles (family, career, eldercare) with which to contend. Half of caregivers had a chronic health problem and one in eight were judged to be 'frail.' On average, caregivers rated their health as good on a scale of excellent, very good, good, fair, and poor.

Both caregivers and clients of adult day programs in Alberta reported satisfaction with the programs. Both appreciated the opportunity for the senior to socialize and found it beneficial. Caregivers also appreciated the respite (the break from caregiving responsibilities) and felt that the senior's health was improved through participation in the programs.

Keating and Munro (1991; Munro, et al., 1995) studied farming families across Alberta and the process of retirement. They conducted face-to-face interviews in 1990 with 74 farm families in which the parent generation was 50 to 65 or so years of age. The researchers interviewed each parent, one child involved in the farming operation, and his/her spouse. In other words, they interviewed the "retiring generation" and the "receiving generation" in order to examine the process by which the farm is transferred from one generation to the next. Keating and Munro found that the retiring generation reported low levels of stress, was working well with the receiving generation, and was handling the farm transfer process well.

In 1989, the Alberta Indian Health Care Commission (no date) conducted a survey of Indian Elders living on reserves in Alberta. The survey examined living, social, and economic circumstances, utilization of health services, and health and disability status. A total of 79 surveys were returned. Almost half indicated that they were not satisfied with their present living arrangements.

In the early 1990s, a team of researchers at the University of Lethbridge (Brown, Buchignani, and Armstrong-Esther) conducted 848 face-to-face interviews across Alberta with Albertans who saw themselves as Aboriginal and who were 50 or more years of age. This study focused on seniors' personally-expressed health and social needs. Detailed analyses were forthcoming at the time of writing.

In the fall of 1991, The Premier's Council in Support of Alberta Families (1991) brought 57 delegates to Edmonton from Indian and Metis communities across Alberta. Regarding the role of elders, the report notes that "Elders are seen as essential in transmitting Native culture and tradition. Participants emphasized the need to keep the elders with the families . . . . Elders were identified as a potential resource to provide foster care or to adopt children when there are problems in the extended family" (p. 6). It was also noted that "Elder care homes are needed in the community because elders lose their spirit very quickly when they are sent out of the community for care" (p. 19).

From 1991 to 1993, over 130 meetings were held across Alberta with First Nations, Metis settlements, and friendship centres to "seek out, hear, and record what Aboriginal people in Alberta thought about their health and the health of their communities" (Aboriginal Health Unit, Alberta Health, no date:i). The report noted the special role of elders in Aboriginal communities. Problems such as poor living conditions (running water, plumbing, electricity), difficulties accessing needed health care, and elder abuse (particularly financial abuse of the senior's old age pension) and neglect were discussed (p. 23-25). Regarding institutional care, the report stated that "Without nursing homes and lodges in communities, most elders face the horrible prospect of being sent away from families, friends, and spiritual homeland to die among strangers" (p. 23). An "Aboriginal Health Strategy," dated 1995, was appended to the report.

Some surveys of Albertans have included seniors as well as non-seniors. For example, the 1990 Alberta Heart Health Survey studied risk factors for cardio-vascular disease in Alberta (Alberta Health, 1991). A total of 2241 persons aged 18-74 participated, including 378 persons 65-74 years of age. Subjects were selected randomly from 13 of Alberta's 27 Health Units. Seniors were more likely than non-seniors to have or to be treated for high blood pressure (29% of males and 39% of females 65-74 years of age). Seniors were more likely to have higher plasma cholesterol, LDL-cholesterol, triglycerides, and higher ratios of plasma cholesterol to HDL-cholesterol. Seniors were less likely to smoke cigarettes or to drink alcohol and were more likely to exercise at least three times a week.

In 1992, a public opinion poll was conducted with a random sample of 1000 Albertans 45 years of age or older (Alberta Ministry Responsible for Seniors, 1992: Appendix F). This poll sought opinions regarding current and future issues concerning seniors in Alberta. The most important issues facing seniors in Alberta were said to be income security, health care, and housing, in that order. Respondents aged 45 to 64 were more concerned about these issues than persons 65 and older. Two-thirds of respondents felt that "there will be insufficient money for government to take care of seniors in ten years" and most felt that there will not be "enough people working to sustain seniors' pensions in the future" (p. F/4). Accordingly, three out of every four respondents said that "seniors will be worse off in a decade than they are now" (p. F/3).

Local surveys of seniors in Alberta will be discussed separately for Edmonton, Calgary, Northern Alberta, Central Alberta, and Southern Alberta. For summaries of a number of these studies (up to 1986), see Hohn (1986b), McQ Enterprises (1986), and Merrett (1986).

Surveys of Seniors in Edmonton

In 1956-57, James (1964) surveyed over 700 seniors living in Edmonton including 40 seniors living in institutions. He found that

. . . the older persons in the sample seem to fare pretty well as judged by conventional standards: most of them own their homes, are not disabled by serious physical difficulties, nor have they spent a great amount of time in hospital; most of the sample maintain a large degree of independence, carry on active lives, and economically are not severe hardship cases.

In spite of generally healthy appearances, however, there are evident social problems. . . . people . . . who do not have independence, who live in substandard conditions, and who live alone and lack close relationships are the ones of concern. . . . While noting with satisfaction the number who seem relatively well off, one should not lose sight of those individuals who are experiencing difficulties. (pp. 123-124)

Most respondents indicated that, in the event that they should have difficulty living independently, they would prefer to remain in their own residence with housekeeping and nursing services provided (p. 132). Should they have to give up their own homes, respondents indicated a preference for a separate cottage, apartment suite, or private room. The findings of this 1956-57 survey are striking in their similarity to survey results obtained 30 and 40 years later.

In 1972, Snider (1973; 1976) surveyed 428 non-institutionalized seniors living in Edmonton, examining health status, need for health care services, and utilization of health care services. Snider pointed out that while seniors are not a homogeneous category, generally most report good morale, good health, and adequate health care services. Snider noted that the physician was seen to be the main "point of entry" to the health care system.

In 1973, a committee made up of representatives of various senior citizens' organizations in Edmonton surveyed 317 non-institutionalized seniors regarding their housing needs (Hannochko, 1974). The majority reported that they were healthy, happy, had adequate income, and were satisfied with their housing. The great majority wanted to remain where they were and would move only for health reasons. Seniors preferred to maintain their independence and, should institutional housing be required, preferred private rooms.

In 1978 the Alberta Alcoholism and Drug Abuse Commission conducted a survey of 584 non-institutionalized seniors living in Edmonton (Sawka, 1978). This study found that almost one-third of seniors did not drink at all and that those who did drink tended to be temperate "social" drinkers. Virtually none of the seniors interviewed were found to use alcohol as a means of dealing with their personal problems in their older years (for similar findings, see also Angus Reid Associates, 1986).

In 1979, 440 non-institutionalized Edmontonians 18 years of age and older (including 87 persons 50-64 years of age and 32 persons 65 and older) were asked about life's satisfactions and pressures (Northcott, 1982). This study found that older respondents were more likely than younger respondents to report no major source of pressure in their lives and were also more likely to report less pressure from various areas of life (except health, where there was no statistically significant difference in reported pressure). Further, older respondents were more likely to report satisfaction with various aspects of life (except health and family life, where there were no statistically significant differences in reported satisfaction). In short, persons in their older years appeared to experience relatively low pressure and relatively high satisfaction.

Two related needs-assessment surveys of non-institutionalized persons 55 years of age and older were conducted in North Edmonton in 1979 and 1981 (North Edmonton Services for People Association, 1981). Generally, respondents were found to be relatively self-sufficient, although some required assistance with heavier tasks (such as snow shovelling). A similar study of 198 non-institutionalized persons 60 years of age and older was conducted in about 1982 in West Central Edmonton (Edmonton Social Services, Westmount Centre, n.d.). The majority of respondents had good social supports, and while awareness of services provided by Edmonton Social Services was low, the great majority stated that they did not need assistance. A few required help with heavier tasks such as snow shovelling. The greatest need for services was found among persons who lived alone, had lower incomes, and were older in age.

A 1983-86 study of the prevalence of psychiatric disorders in Edmonton (Bland, et al., 1988) interviewed 3258 non-institutionalized persons 18 years of age and older including 358 persons 65+ years of age and found that psychiatric prevalence rates were generally lower in the elderly than in the general population, except for rates of cognitive impairment, which were higher. This study also examined a sample of 199 elderly institutionalized persons. While about 3.5% of the non-institutionalized seniors were found to suffer mild cognitive impairment and none were severely impaired, over one-third of institutionalized seniors were severely impaired and another one-third suffered mild impairment.

Cognitive impairment was found to be a major reason for the institutionalization of seniors, with risk of impairment increasing with age.

In 1988, LaRocque, et al. (1988) surveyed 100 inner city residents in Edmonton 55 years of age and older. The majority of these respondents were males who were not currently married, rented their accommodation, and had few personal resources (e.g., low income, poor health). Nonetheless, respondents were fiercely independent and managed as best they could. Institutionalization was resisted and was seen as an undesirable alternative. Respondents preferred to live independently.

Open-ended interviews were conducted in 1988 with a non-random sample of 118 seniors in the Mill Creek District of Edmonton, an area with a higher than average concentration of seniors (Edmonton Social Services, Mill Creek Centre, 1989). Most of the respondents lived in their own homes, while a few lived in seniors' apartments or in seniors' lodges. Socially isolated frail seniors appeared to be very rare. Most seniors appeared satisfied with their current situation.

A survey of 195 South Asians aged 50 and older was conducted in Edmonton in 1995 (Bassi, 1995). The great majority of the respondents identified with the Sikh religion and indicated that Punjabi was their mother tongue. The culture of South Asians emphasizes strong family ties. Many of the respondents had come to Canada to join their younger family members. While the majority had incomes below the poverty line, nevertheless, most had free room and board with their children or grandchildren and received moral as well as financial support. There was no indication that residences were crowded. Most rated their health as excellent or good, as opposed to fair, poor, or very poor. One in three said that their health was worse than it was five years ago. Most enjoyed a good to fair quality of life. It was recommended that the South Asians "should emulate the lead given by the Chinese Community and work to provide ethno-cultural based Nursing-cum-Assisted Living Facilities for their community" (p. 20).

Surveys of Seniors in Calgary

In 1971, the Senior Citizens' Central Council of Calgary initiated a non-random survey of 959 non-institutionalized senior Calgarians (Fuez, 1972). Most respondents indicated that they were in good health and were not dependent on the care of others. In 1977, a sample of 305 of the 4550 persons on the waiting list for senior citizen housing in Calgary was interviewed (Alberta Housing and Public Works, 1977). A considerable number of persons indicated that, while their present housing was satisfactory, they were on the waiting list "just in case." The majority of respondents were over 70 years of age, female, not currently married, renters, in good health, but with low incomes. One-bedroom units were preferred to bachelor suites. The main reasons given for wanting to move were high rents (for those renting in the private marketplace) and difficulty maintaining own home.

In 1979, a random sample of 122 senior citizen lodge residents in Calgary was interviewed along with a sample of 138 "potential" lodge residents (seniors in subsidized housing or receiving Meals on Wheels) (deCocq and Macleod, 1980).

Lodge residents were predominantly female, not currently married (mostly widowed), and had a median age of 79. The most frequent reasons given for moving to the lodge included medical problems, difficulties managing daily tasks, and a desire to be independent and have their own room. Most residents were satisfied with the various aspects of lodge living. The majority of potential lodge residents had not seriously considered moving to a lodge and many said that they knew very little about the lodges. Respondents felt that the least desirable aspects of lodge living would be sharing a room with a stranger and, accordingly, rated a private room as a highly desirable feature. Most felt that government should help seniors to remain in their own houses.

In 1982, a non-random sample of 500 Calgarians aged 65 and older living independently or living in senior citizens' housing was interviewed (Calgary Social Services Department, 1983). Most reported good health and satisfaction with the health care system. Most reported that they did not require social services.

A non-random sample of 132 seniors living in housing alternatives ranging from nursing homes to private homes in Calgary was interviewed in about 1984 to assess housing needs and the viability of the shared housing concept (Rutherford, et al., 1985). This study found that there did not appear to be a "housing gap" and that there were many support services facilitating independent living in the community.

A non-random sample of 100 South Asian (including India, Pakistan, Bangladesh, Sri Lanka, and Nepal) seniors 55 years of age and older and living in Calgary was interviewed in 1986 (Dholakia, et al., 1987). Most came to Canada under the sponsorship of their grown children, who had previously immigrated to Canada. Half lived with their extended families, usually in a son's home rather than in a daughter's home. Many preferred to live independently. Problems identified include lack of proficiency in English, which constituted a barrier to social participation, and underemployment, which was a frequent problem for those seniors who would have liked to work in their professions and trades. The younger generations tended to assimilate culturally more than the older generation.

In 1987, a random sample of 148 Chinese, mostly non-institutionalized seniors (some lived in senior citizen residences – Oi Kwan Place or Oi Kwan Manor) 60 years of age and older living in Calgary were surveyed (Oi Kwan Foundation, 1988). Eighty-five percent had been born in China and about two-thirds had come to Canada to join their grown children who had immigrated previously. Respondents with a spouse said that if they were to have difficulty looking after themselves they would mostly prefer to remain at home and be cared for by their spouse. Moving in with family was seen as less desirable than having caregivers come into their home or than moving into an institution. Respondents indicated that having their own room, Chinese-speaking staff, Chinese meals, and a convenient location would be important considerations if they had to choose a nursing home.

In 1991, elderly Chinese immigrants were surveyed in Calgary (Lai and McDonald, 1995). A random sample was selected from elders living in three senior housing facilities for the Chinese in downtown Calgary. Virtually all of the seniors interviewed had been born in Mainland China and over half had immigrated to Canada from Hong Kong. Most were widows. Two-thirds lived alone while the remainder lived with their spouse. Only a few were fluent in English. All depended on the Old Age Pension and/or social welfare. Nevertheless, most reported that they had sufficient financial resources. Further, the Chinese elderly immigrants in this study were reported to be quite satisfied with their lives.

Calgary Health Services (1995) reported on the health of Calgarians and also on the results of a survey of 450 seniors conducted in 1995. Almost two-thirds of seniors reported very good or excellent health and almost three-quarters indicated that they had no limitations in their daily activities. This study reported that almost a third of seniors in Calgary had lost all of their natural teeth.

In 1995, 111 female and 18 male clients of the Kerby Seniors Centre in Calgary were involved in a project which addressed violence in older families (Boyack, et al., 1995). The study group consisted of persons 50 years of age and older (mean age 72) who had sought assistance from the Kerby Centre regarding violent family relationships. The "perpetrator" of the violence was usually either a spouse (in 42% of the cases) or an adult child (32%). In-depth information was obtained from 10 clients who told their "stories" in detail. The forms of violence reported included material/financial abuse, physical violence, psychological abuse, violation of civil or human rights, and neglect.

Surveys of Seniors in Northern Alberta

In 1971, 94 seniors living independently in the Lesser Slave Lake rural area were interviewed (Alberta Human Resources Development Authority, 1971). The major concerns expressed were for more social and recreational opportunities and for transportation, the lack of which was a hindrance to socializing. In 1974, virtually all of the persons aged 60 and older (n=393) were surveyed in the Smoky River Municipal District (Smoky River M.D., Family Service Bureau, 1974). Most respondents were francophone. Most lived in the district's towns. While most were in good health and were able to live independently, most said that they did not want to live with their offspring and there was an indication that accommodation in the lodge or nursing home was preferred. A similar survey was conducted in Smokey River in 1978 when 422 persons aged 65 and older were interviewed (Smokey River M.D., Preventive Social Services, 1979). While most lived independently in their own homes, 60 resided in lodges. Both groups expressed satisfaction with their accommodation. Forty-three seniors resided in the nursing home (average age 81). Other than those persons in the nursing home, respondents were found to be in generally good health.

In 1986, 350 interviews of institutionalized and non-institutionalized seniors 65 years of age and older were conducted in the more developed areas of the Peace River Health Unit and another 53 interviews were completed in remote communities (mostly with Native seniors) (Regional Interdisciplinary Steering Committee for Geriatric Services in the North Peace River Region, 1986). Those Native seniors in the remote areas expected that their families would care for them should they become dependent and that they would remain in their community. In contrast, non-native seniors preferred not to live with their families should they become dependent but rather preferred to move into a lodge or nursing home located in or as close as possible to their own community. Private rooms were preferred. Respondents were generally satisfied with health care services and with their accommodation (whether farm, home in town, seniors' apartment, lodge, or nursing home). Some expressed an interest in domestic assistance (e.g., snow shovelling).

In 1988, an attempt was made to interview face-to-face all 203 seniors in the City of Fort McMurray. A total of 141 interviews were completed. (In addition, 370 questionnaires were completed by employees aged 50 to 64 working for major employers in the City.) The "average" senior was female, 72 years of age, married, had no immediate plans to move, had family contact daily, and was in reasonably good health. The majority of seniors felt that their present income was adequate, but some expressed uncertainty as to their financial future. Finally, most seniors preferred to live independently in their own homes. Should that not become possible, seniors preferred "whatever housing style gives them as much independence as possible along with the support they need. Most respondents did not want to rely on their families for support" (City of Fort McMurray, 1988).

Surveys of Seniors in Central Alberta

In 1970, 1157 persons aged 65 and older living in the County of Lacombe were surveyed (Lacombe Council on Aging, 1971). The great majority lived independently in their own homes (about 10% lived in a lodge or nursing home) and did not require either medical, personal, or housekeeping services. In 1975, 436 seniors were surveyed in the Municipal District of Provost (Maier, 1975). Ninety-four percent reported no need for medical treatment other than that which was currently utilized or available. Most lived in their own homes; about 20% rented apartments or lived in the lodge or nursing home. Virtually all were satisfied with their present living situation. Some indicated that assistance with home maintenance, housekeeping and/or transportation, and/or home nursing services would help them remain in their own homes and that they were willing to pay modest charges for such services. (A similar survey conducted in 1982 produced consistent findings – see Gregory, 1982).

In 1977, all households with telephones in the County of Strathcona (excluding Fort Saskatchewan) were telephoned to identify all physically disabled persons and all persons 60 years of age and older (Lawrence, 1977). This survey focused on the transportation needs of seniors and the disabled. While the majority did not require assistance, some indicated that they would make use of volunteer drivers, if such a service was made available.

In 1980, 97 seniors (aged 65+) living independently in the town of Ponoka were interviewed (Blair, 1981). In addition, 48 people who served as central informal (unpaid) resources to these seniors filled out a questionnaire. The great majority of rural seniors were found to be healthy and in little need of assistance. Offspring, other family members, friends, and neighbors were found to be important sources of aid. In 1981, 211 seniors were surveyed in the towns of Grand Centre and Cold Lake (Alberta Council on Aging, 1983). This survey identified such problems as the high cost of heating fuel and the need for a nursing home in the area. In 1982, 115 seniors (65+ years of age) in Camrose, living independently in their homes or in seniors housing, were interviewed face-to-face (Krismer, 1982). Most reported good health and a desire to remain in their own homes as long as possible.

In 1983, 1366 persons 65+ years of age and living in their own homes or in senior citizens' apartments (lodge residents were not interviewed) in the Minburn-Vermilion Health Unit were interviewed face-to-face (Zoerb, 1983). Most did not require any services to help them remain in their own homes. Those requiring assistance most often listed home maintenance, housekeeping, home nursing care, and transportation as desired services. Most were willing to pay a modest fee for these services. Most reported relatively good health and indicated that they were able to care for themselves.

In 1983, all of the elders (60+ years of age; n=25) of the Frog Lake Band were interviewed (Frog Lake Band Family and Community Support Services, 1983). Most lived with spouse or family. Most had, at their request, grandchildren living with them. Any housing, such as a senior citizens lodge, which separated Native seniors from their community or which did not allow for the accommodation of grandchildren was seen as unacceptable. It was expected and preferred that elders would be cared for by their own families, when necessary, except when serious medical treatment was required. There appeared to be a need for home improvements, transportation, and a seniors' centre. Native elders were perceived to be a group "that does not complain."

In 1986, 66 seniors living in their own homes or in seniors' housing in the town of Hanna were interviewed (Author Unknown, 1986). Most were able to care for themselves and most did not use or need available services. In 1986, 548 interviews were conducted with most of the persons 55 years of age and older (including 237 persons 65 years of age and older) in the Hinton area (Taylor, 1986). Most respondents were healthy and most felt that their medical, financial, social, and transportation needs were adequately met. Most preferred to remain in their own homes and valued their independence. In the event of failing health, most preferred home care services. Seniors did not want to be forced to leave the community by failing health and wished to see a nursing home and/or seniors' lodge built in Hinton, although few would live in these facilities unless forced to do so. Most preferred not to move in with their children as they did not want to be a burden to them.

In 1987, 563 interviews were conducted with most of the persons 55 years of age and older (including 333 persons aged 65+) in the Elk Point Hospital District (Stone, n.d.). Most respondents reported reasonably good health, had frequent contact with family members, preferred to remain independently in their own homes, and did not wish to rely on their families for support should they no longer be able to live independently. The majority preferred either seniors' lodges or home care services in the event that they should require assistance.

A 1988 survey of all seniors living in the city of Fort Saskatchewan repeats a similar 1982 survey (Higham, 1988). There were 544 respondents in 1988 including lodge and nursing home residents. While most lived independently, acceptable preferred housing options (other than own home) included seniors' apartments, lodges, and maintained semi-detached housing (e.g., Horizon Village concept). Services that would assist seniors to stay in their own homes included help with heavier housekeeping and yardwork.

Forbes (1994) interviewed 46 of the 122 individuals on the regional wait list for long term care (LTC) facility placement and 46 of the 61 "light care" residents in the six long term facilities in the Vegreville Region. Fifty percent of the light care residents in long term care were 86 years of age or older. Almost the same percentage of individuals on the waiting list were 86+ years of age. While 52% of those on the waiting list said that their health was very good or good, one in six reported very poor health and most of these persons were willing to be admitted immediately to a LTC facility. Another one in six on the waiting list said that they did not presently require placement, but were on the list "in case." While long term care involves formal support, nevertheless, informal (unpaid) support, usually from family members, was also extensive.

Surveys of Seniors in Southern Alberta

In 1974, a random sample of 482 institutionalized and non-institutionalized, rural and urban, persons 65 years of age and older living in Calgary, Nanton, and Drumheller and district was interviewed (Birch and Koroluk, 1974). The majority of respondents were satisfied with their present lifestyle. The institutionalized were less likely to be satisfied with their current activities, more likely to have poorer health, and were more likely to be dissatisfied with their housing arrangements.

In 1977, 1662 retired persons living in their own homes in Medicine Hat were interviewed (Medicine Hat Preventive Social Services Department, n.d.). The great majority did not plan to move within the next five years. About one in five indicated a need for assistance with minor home maintenance (e.g., snow shovelling) and repairs.

In 1980, 216 seniors living independently in the Mount View and Foothills Health Units were interviewed about their general health needs. At the same time, 411 seniors living in their own homes, apartments, seniors' housing, lodges, a nursing home, and an auxiliary hospital in the Mount View Health Unit were interviewed about their mental health needs (Hohn, 1986b:57-59; Merrett, 1986:34-40; Kerr, et al., 1983; Thurston, et al., 1982). Respondents were found to be generally healthy and satisfied with life.

In 1981, 45 seniors from Brooks, Medicine Hat, and Edmonton returned a mailed survey questionnaire as part of a Red Cross study (national sample=775) (McQ Enterprises, 1986:20). The results of this study are considered unreliable for Albertans due to the small number of respondents.

In 1981, 501 seniors in the town of High River were surveyed (Alberta Council on Aging, 1983). The survey identified issues such as problems with housing, inflation, and need for a local bus depot. In 1983, 315 seniors and 263 "pre-retired adults" living in Medicine Hat returned a mail questionnaire (Associated Planning Consultants, 1983). The range of existing services for seniors was found to be largely satisfactory.

In 1986, a non-random sample of seniors was interviewed in the communities of Coleman, Bellevue, and Blairmore (Hohn, 1986b:28). Many seniors themselves were found to be caregivers for an elderly or disabled person. Almost one half expressed interest in a moderately priced handyman service.

Conclusions Arising from the Surveys of Elderly Albertans

One of the most striking observations arising from this review of surveys of seniors in Alberta is the consistency of findings. It seems to matter little whether the study was done recently or twenty or more years ago, or whether respondents live in a large city, a small town, a rural area, or in the north, centre, or south of the province. Wherever and whenever surveyed, the great majority of seniors are found to be generally healthy, happy, and living independently. Seniors prefer to remain in their own houses and, should the need arise, welcome services designed to help them remain at home and maintain their independence. Seniors often speak of the difficulty of managing the heavier household tasks (such as snow shovelling) and welcome moderately priced home help services. Just the same, the great majority of seniors have frequent contact with family members and other persons and, when help is needed, frequently receive assistance from family, friends, and/or neighbors. In the event that a person can no longer live independently, the great majority of seniors say that they would prefer accommodation in a senior citizens' apartment, senior citizens' lodge, or long term care facility located in their own community. Most prefer not to live with their children because they do not want to be a burden to them. Should institutional accommodation become necessary, there is a strong preference for a private room.

In short, most seniors do not admit to unmet needs. On the one hand, seniors appear to have fewer "needs" than the stereotypes imply. On the other hand, Alberta's service delivery system is perceived to be generally adequate and seniors tend to be satisfied with the services that they do utilize. The stereotype of older Albertans as sick, disabled, dependent, socially isolated, lonely, and demoralized simply has no validity. Given the consistency of survey results, there is really little need for additional general surveys of seniors. Each general survey simply serves to further invalidate the stereotype.

What is needed now are studies that target "at risk" or "needy" groups of seniors, although these groups are relatively small in size and not always easily identified. Future studies should target older seniors (above the age of 84, for example), frail seniors (whether young-old or old-old), the dying, the socially isolated, the most poor, seniors who are recent immigrants, and seniors with specific chronic conditions such as diabetes, foot problems, arthritis, dementia, or the sequelae from stroke. Future studies should focus on these selected target groups both in the community and in institutional care facilities and should examine not only the seniors themselves but also their informal and formal caregivers as well.

This review shows that surveys of seniors in the community have been fairly common. Client surveys have also been quite common, especially for seniors in lodges and long term care facilities. While formal evaluations of programs for seniors may have also been conducted, these are often done "in-house" and do not necessarily become part of the public literature. It has been argued that future studies of seniors might do well to move away from general community surveys and client surveys to more targeted research. This targeted research could benefit from a wider variety of methods. For example, unstructured, in-depth interviews would yield rich, qualitative data to complement the quantitative data obtained from the many structured survey questionnaires.

While there are many issues of importance still requiring further consideration, it is important to remember that, generally speaking, the great majority of seniors in Alberta are healthy, happy, and able to live independently or with a modest amount of assistance from family, friends, neighbors, and formal support services. Despite the statistics that tell us that seniors make up the bulk of the residents of long term care facilities and despite the statistics that tell us that seniors use disproportionate amounts of physician services, hospital resources, and home care, it is important to note that most seniors live independently and utilize medical services infrequently and support services rarely, if at all. In other words, the statistics that fuel the stereotype of the sick and dependent senior citizen arise from the very small proportion of seniors who are indeed greatly disadvantaged. It is perhaps time to concentrate our research attention on those relatively few seniors who are so disadvantaged.

Chapter Four
Issues in Population Aging

Changing demographic profiles are accompanied by and have implications for trends in other aspects of society including politics, economics, public attitudes, and social ideology (Government of Canada, 1982:119-145; Institute for Health Care Facilities of the Future, 1988). This chapter examines various issues related to population aging, focusing on the Canadian context generally and the Alberta context in particular. The implications of these broad societal trends for future service delivery are discussed. This chapter first examines political issues associated with population aging and then goes on to examine economic issues, changing public attitudes, and trends in social ideology.

Political Issues Associated With Population Aging

Voting-Bloc Scenario

As seniors become an increasingly large proportion of the population, it follows that they will also become an increasingly large proportion of the voting public. In the past, seniors have tended to be active in the political process and have had relatively high rates of voter participation (Novak, 1993:409; Government of Canada, 1982:141; for a discussion of the Canadian seniors' movement, see Gifford, 1990). While seniors as a group are heterogeneous and hold a variety of political views, nevertheless, seniors do constitute an important special interest group. As the opposition to the 1985 proposal to partially de-index the Old Age Pension illustrates, seniors can be united by certain issues that threaten their interests and can successfully influence the political process (Novak, 1993:416-418). It seems likely that politicians are increasingly aware of the interests and power of the older age group.

In Alberta, the Provincial Senior Citizens Advisory Council (now the Seniors Advisory Council for Alberta) was established in 1976 to advise government on seniors' issues. The Senior Citizens Bureau (later Secretariat) had been established a year earlier and worked in conjunction with the Advisory Council to provide information to the public on seniors' issues. (The Secretariat was discontinued in 1990 and most of its functions were absorbed by the Council.) Until 1991, the Seniors Advisory Council was housed in the department of government responsible for social services. In 1991, a separate ministry was created responsible for seniors. This new ministry was headed by a Minister Responsible for Seniors (an elected MLA) and by a Deputy Minister (a high ranking civil servant). The Seniors Advisory Council for Alberta reported directly to the Minister Responsible for Seniors. A Seniors Directorate (established in 1990 as the Services to Seniors Division, Family and Social Services) reported to the Deputy Minister Responsible for Seniors and was charged with the development and coordination of governmental policy for the aged. The creation of the Ministry Responsible for Seniors seemed to indicate the government's increasing recognition of seniors and their concerns.

The Ministry for Seniors, however, soon fell victim to the Alberta Government's deficit elimination and debt reduction efforts. In 1993, the Ministry for Seniors was disbanded and the Seniors Advisory Council was assigned to the Department of Community Development.[1] Also in 1993, the Seniors Directorate was disbanded and its functions were assumed by the Department of Community Development. As of 1996, seniors issues and programs were the responsibility of the Seniors Division and its various branches in the Department of Community Development. A toll-free Seniors Information Line, previously managed by the Seniors Advisory Council, was operated by Alberta Community Development. This toll-free service allowed seniors anywhere in the province to phone for information.

The Seniors Advisory Council for Alberta continued to produce an annual report to government with recommendations concerning policies and programs relevant to seniors. The Council also continued to publish an annual edition of a booklet titled *Programs for Seniors*. This publication contains information about benefits and programs available to seniors from various levels of government (local, provincial, federal) and from private agencies.

Given that there will be greater numbers and proportions of seniors in the future, and given that future cohorts of seniors are likely to be increasingly well-educated, financially better-off, and healthier, it follows that seniors will be an increasingly salient factor in both provincial and federal politics. Indeed, one extreme scenario predicts a "war" of sorts between the generations as seniors demand and win more and more social and economic benefits from governments while non-elderly taxpayers become increasingly resentful of the tax burden that they are forced to shoulder. This "war-between-the-generations" scenario assumes that there will be a widespread perception among the non-elderly citizenry that society cannot afford to support a large dependent senior population. A less extreme scenario suggests that seniors may win a partial transfer of social resources from the declining segment of young people to the growing group of seniors. While this "redistribution-of-resources" scenario assumes that society can ease economic pressures by reassigning resources, such a transfer may generate opposition from parents of young children, for example, and/or from the education lobby or day care interest groups.

Equity Scenario

The House of Commons Standing Committee on Human Rights recommended in 1988 (Stackhouse) that age discrimination be eliminated in Canada. Such political initiatives are likely to be welcomed by seniors and may indeed remove certain social practices that socially and economically disadvantage many seniors. This humanitarian search for equality may allow seniors to retire, for example, when they choose and may thereby increase seniors' self-reliance and independence. Nevertheless, ironically, the pursuit of equity may be used as a political justification for eliminating age-based programs such as old age security, which single out seniors for benefits that are not available to non-seniors. For example, the elimination of age discrimination may result in the elimination of mandatory retirement. This in turn may lead to an expectation that people work to support themselves as long as possible, relying on social welfare, unemployment insurance, and/or medicare should they become unemployed or too incapacitated to work. In other words, under this scenario, the entire old age security program could be eliminated and replaced at substantially less cost with an extension of those programs now designed for disadvantaged non-elderly persons (e.g., social assistance and unemployment insurance). Instead of paying pensions for life to retired workers, pension programs could be recast as unemployment and disability insurance to protect older workers who lose their jobs for either economic or health reasons.

Summary

In summary, seniors in the future may have the political clout to win an extension of present benefit programs, or may at least continue to maintain present benefits. Alternatively, a political emphasis on the elimination of age discrimination may result in some benefit programs being curtailed or even eliminated. Governments have an interest in both scenarios. Given that governments are concerned with maintaining political power (i.e., winning elections), it follows that governments will tend to cater to influential interest groups, including seniors. However, it is not clear that seniors' interests will necessarily win out over other interests. Given that governments are concerned not only with maintaining power but also with balancing budgets, it follows that an emphasis on the elimination of "age discrimination," while appearing to seek social justice, might also serve to redefine old age and reduce the economic obligations of governments to older persons. Whatever political scenario one envisions for the future, it is assumed that economic considerations will play an important role in the politics of population aging.

Economic Issues Associated With Population Aging

Bankruptcy Scenario

Since the mid-1970s, the federal government has had large annual budget deficits and has accumulated a debt totaling some $578 billion as of early 1996. This is the equivalent of almost $20 000 for every man, woman, and child in Canada. In 1995-96, some $47 billion, an amount larger than the annual deficit, was spent on interest payments for the national debt (Department of Finance Canada, 1996; Edmonton Journal, 3 March 1996:F1). Indeed, interest payments made up roughly one-third of Canada's annual expenditure in 1995-96 and this proportion has been growing with the rising national debt. Furthermore, the Province of Alberta had budget deficits every year from 1985/86 through the

1993/94 fiscal year (Alberta Treasury, 1994 and 1995). Alberta's total gross debt was $32.5 billion in early 1996 (about $11 600 per person). The net debt, which takes into account assets such as the Heritage Fund, is much lower – $12.7 billion in early 1995 (Edmonton Journal, 23 February 1996:A1; A4; see also 27 June 1996:A8; Alberta Treasury, 1995). In 1996/97, $1.4 billion was to be spent on interest payments on the accumulated debt.

The string of deficits and the accumulated debt have resulted in pressure to raise taxes on the one hand and, on the other hand, to reduce expenditures. Raising taxes has never been popular and the spectre of a tax revolt or of a public backlash at election time makes politicians nervous. However, cutting services also tends to be unpopular and so politicians are caught in a catch-22, damned if they raise taxes, damned if they cut services, and damned by rising debts if they do neither. The aging of the population exacerbates concern over the economy because of fears that the increase in seniors will cause service costs to rise. The gloomiest scenario envisions demographic aging forcing up costs and outstripping the economy's ability to pay. Swamped by mountainous debt and crushing interest payments, the economy collapses into bankruptcy.

There are really three "villains" in this bankruptcy scenario: population aging, federal and provincial budgetary deficits, and high interest rates. Actually, most analysts today believe that the demographic pressures themselves are not that severe and project that costs will rise only moderately as a result of population aging per se (Barer, Evans, and Hertzman, 1995; Black, et al., 1995; Denton and Spencer, 1995; Marzouk, 1991; Denton, Feaver, and Spencer, 1987 and 1986; Evans, 1987a and 1987b; Messinger and Powell, 1987; Denton, Li, and Spencer, 1987; Barer, et al., 1986 and 1987; McDaniel, 1986:53-56; Foot, 1982; Stone and Fletcher, 1980; Denton and Spencer, 1980a and 1980b; Powell and Martin, 1980; Stone and MacLean, 1979; for less optimistic analyses, see Henripin, 1994, and Burke, 1991). The problem is that these moderate increases in costs, coupled with rising total debt and high interest rates, might constitute the proverbial "straw" that breaks the economy's back, or in the very least, makes a bad situation worse.

The bankruptcy scenario tends to focus simplistically on demographic aging as the factor driving up future costs. Another version of the bankruptcy scenario focuses not only on the population aging trend, but also considers trends in the utilization and cost of services consumed by seniors. In the area of health care, for example, trends such as the development of new and expensive technologies, inflation in the cost of medical supplies and provider incomes, and more intensive usage of the health care delivery system (whether client-initiated or provider-initiated or both) are expected to drive up future health care costs independently of the population aging trend. In short, this version of the bankruptcy scenario suggests that an economic crisis may result as a consequence of a growing number of seniors making increasingly intensive usage (of their own volition and/or on the recommendation of service providers) of increasingly costly services. This version of the bankruptcy scenario suggests that a future crisis can be averted by "shifting the emphasis" (Health and Welfare Canada, 1986) to less costly services, a strategy which is being actively promoted by the Alberta Government.

Improving-Economic-Situation Scenario

An alternative scenario envisions the elimination of annual deficits and a time of reducing or at least "growing" our way out of our total debt (in time, it is hoped that the economy will expand, the population will grow implying an increasing tax base, and the total debt will deflate in value assuming that interest is paid regularly and no other debt is added to the total). Under this scenario, the costs of supporting an increasing senior population are met by an improving economic situation and, at worst, by modest increases in taxation.

Less-for-More Scenario

It is often assumed that budgets will not be balanced unless taxes are raised and expenditures reduced. Increased taxes, "temporary" surcharges, the Goods and Services Tax (GST), elimination of certain tax deductions (e.g., the $1000 interest income deduction), increases in the contribution rate for the Canada Pension Plan and repayment by the better-off of Old Age Security (the so-called "clawback") have been coupled with discussions of funding restraint for various social programs. In short, recent attempts to raise revenues are being followed by substantial cuts in social service expenditures.

Add-On Scenario

The current emphasis on maintaining seniors' independence and on preventing or forestalling institutionalization can be viewed as attempts to reduce service costs. Usually these reforms are justified on both humanitarian and economic grounds. Consider home care for example. This program is designed to maintain seniors' independence by forestalling or preventing institutionalization. It is argued that this program will not only improve the quality of seniors' lives but will also be cheaper than institutional care. If successful, this movement might well improve the lives and prospects of seniors and at the same time help society extricate itself from its economic difficulties. However, there is a concern that the costs of promoting seniors' health, fostering independence, and preventing institutionalization will be **additional to** the present costs of supporting dependent elderly persons (Chappell, 1987:501; Chappell, et al., 1986:99, 110, 141; Schwenger and Gross, 1980:225; Soderstrom, 1978:52-56). In other words, services designed to prevent or forestall institutionalization and thereby designed to reduce overall costs might actually **increase** overall costs **unless** institutional beds are actually closed, a decision which health care workers and local communities often resist. Nevertheless, this is exactly the strategy which the Alberta Government implemented in the mid-1990s when institutional beds were closed so that funding could be shifted to community-based care while at the same time reducing total costs.

Volunteer Scenario

The current emphasis on reducing usage of expensive facility-based services emphasizes individual self-reliance on the one hand, but also on the other hand emphasizes interdependence with family, friends, neighbors, community, and professional service providers (see, for example, Health and Welfare Canada, 1986:4). In other words, the community-based service model that is currently being advocated by both the provincial and federal governments relies to a degree on, and is in part less expensive because of, volunteer support (Jefferys, 1983).

In the past, the great majority of care provided in the home by "volunteer" family members has been provided by females (Keating, et al., 1994; Connidis, 1989:49-50; Gee and Kimball, 1987:86-87). While service delivery in the future may rely increasingly on the contributions of volunteers, it is not at all clear that women in the future will be either able or willing to volunteer these anticipated services (Gee, 1990:197; Myles, 1991). As women increasingly pursue careers outside of the home, they are less able to provide care in the home for dependent family members. Further, as women increasingly earn recognition and remuneration in formal careers, the expectation that some women should volunteer their labor without remuneration, with little if any recognition, and at some cost in terms of lost opportunities may become increasingly unacceptable. Taking an optimistic point of view, the emerging ideals of egalitarianism in the family may result in a more equitable sharing among males and females of the burden of caring for dependent family members. On the other hand, a more pessimistic view suggests that in the future neither males nor females may be available or willing to provide needed volunteer services. This would tend to lead to a "crisis in care giving" (Myles, 1991).

Shortages of Services in Rural Areas Scenario

The general movement of the population from rural to urban areas means that seniors may be left in rural areas with reduced informal supports, for example, as family members move away. Furthermore, some rural areas in Alberta have had a continuing difficulty attracting and retaining formal supports such as health care personnel. It follows that the service needs of seniors in some rural areas of the province, at least, may become increasingly problematic.

Redefinition-of-Old-Age Scenario

One extreme scenario suggests that old age might be redefined as a social category, perhaps replaced by the concept of "frailty," for example. Such a redefinition, especially if coupled with an increased emphasis on the idea of individual self-reliance, might result in an expectation that individuals be productive taxpaying members of society as long as possible whether at the age of 65, 75, or 85. Dependency on the public purse would be justified only by "frailty," implying an inability to work and care for oneself because of poor health and/or disability. Such a development would be viewed as a victory by both the proponents of individual self-reliance and the opponents of mandatory retirement and age discrimination. Those looking forward to a life of pensioned leisure after the age of 65 would not be pleased should anticipated rewards fail to materialize.

A variation on this theme involves the restructuring of the life course. Instead of eliminating retirement all together, retirement could be "redistributed" (Myles and Street, 1995). Instead of the "school followed by work followed by retirement" life course, periods of temporary retirement could be used in mid-career for education/retraining, childcare, eldercare, recreation/leisure, and so on.

A less extreme version of the redefinition-of-old-age scenario involves raising the age of entitlement for old age benefits. Brown (1991:111, 119-120) observes that this is being considered in many nations. Indeed, the United States plans to raise the normal retirement age slowly from age 65 to age 67 over a 25-year period beginning in 2002. Brown further argues that by raising the age of eligibility for government-sponsored retirement income security in Canada from age 65 in 2006 to age 69 in 2030, the costs of supporting the aging population could be managed without any additional burden on the taxpayer.

Summary

In summary, one can envision a number of different scenarios regarding both provincial and federal economic futures. Budgetary deficits and large accumulated governmental debts together with the aging of the population and rising service costs (e.g., per capita health care costs) imply an increasing inability to pay for social programs in the future. High levels of taxation will tend to be coupled with reductions in services. Certainly there is an ongoing attempt to shift from expensive services to less expensive alternatives (e.g., from facility-based care to community-based care and from "dependency" to "independence" and "self-reliance"). The extent to which the increased emphasis on self-reliance and on community-based care will actually reduce overall costs remains to be seen. Furthermore, the extent of the availability of volunteer supports in the future may or may not be sufficient to guarantee the practical and economic success of the self-reliance and community-based care philosophy. Finally, it is important to note that the economic future is likely to depend more on trends in service delivery than on population aging per se.

Public Attitudes and the Aging of the Population

Stereotypes and Agism

Public attitudes towards old age often reflect widely-held cultural stereotypes. A stereotype is an erroneous generalization about social group, for example, "old people are poor," or "sick," or "lonely." Such statements imply that all old people are disadvantaged, or at least that the majority are. While some seniors are disadvantaged, the majority are not. Nevertheless, there is a tendency to assume that seniors are worse off than they really are. A national study conducted in the United States asked seniors and non-seniors how problematic were various aspects of life in old age (Harris, 1975). This study found that seniors reported life in old age to be far less problematic than non-seniors perceived it to be.

The stereotypes associated with old age tend to reflect themes of dependency, incompetence, and irrelevancy. Old age is often equated with dependency because of stereotypes that emphasize poor health, physical disability, cognitive impairment, poverty, and widowhood. Dependency implies an inability to take care of oneself, or in other words, incompetence. In addition, incompetence is associated with old age because of stereotypes that emphasize slowness, rigidity, obsolescence, inefficiency, and lack of productivity. Finally, old age may seem irrelevant given a socio-cultural emphasis on youthful vitality and middle-aged prime. In short, old age is devalued and stigmatized. Goffman (1963) defines a stigma as "an attribute that is deeply discrediting" (p. 3) and defines stigmatization as being "disqualified from full social acceptance" (preface). Accordingly, there is a tendency to discredit, disqualify, overlook, and ignore seniors.

Old, dependent, incompetent, and irrelevant – these cultural perceptions of seniors suggest that the elderly population is victimized by agism. Agism refers to prejudicial attitudes and discriminatory behaviors that are based solely on age. Like sexism and racism, agism is becoming increasingly unacceptable. Nevertheless, one still frequently hears it argued in subtle and not so subtle ways that "the old should make way for the young." For example, it might be suggested that older employees should retire so that young people can have the older persons' jobs. It is unacceptable today to suggest that one racial or ethnic group take lesser jobs or forego employment so that another group can obtain employment and, similarly, it is unacceptable to suggest that one sex forego employment or take lesser jobs so that the other sex might find employment. Nevertheless, it is often argued that seniors should give up their jobs to make way for the young. In short, while racism and sexism are unacceptable today, agism still persists.

Given the current emphasis on aging in the newspapers, on television, in the universities and in government, one might assume that in the future the public will be better and better informed about the realities of old age. Myths and stereotypes will be debunked, perhaps, and public attitudes and social practices might well become less and less agist. Such a development might be referred to as the "social enlightenment scenario." Nevertheless, if an aging population is seen as a threat by other segments of society (e.g., younger taxpayers), then negative stereotypes may be retained, fueled by the pejorative rhetoric that tends to accompany social and political struggle. (For a short discussion of the "greedy geezer" and "job snatcher" stereotypes, see McDonald, 1995.) This alternative development might be referred to as the "backlash scenario." In short, while one might hope for a future without negative stereotyping or agism, other less optimistic trends may evolve regarding the ways in which seniors are perceived.

Rising Expectations Scenario

Today's middle-aged baby boomers or young people may have very different expectations for services when they are old than do today's seniors. Indeed, it is often assumed that each successive group of seniors will have higher and higher

and therefore more and more expensive expectations. Under this "rising expectations" scenario, it is assumed that future seniors will expect better pensions,
better health care, better subsidized housing (e.g., more space, more rooms),
better institutional facilities (e.g., private rooms), and so on. Governments which
fail to meet rising expectations will tend to incur political costs unless they can
deflect "blame" away from themselves. Defining a population aging "crisis" and
blaming seniors for the provincial and federal governments' inability to provide
additional services is one way of deflecting blame.

The "I Would Rather Die" Scenario

In contrast to the rising expectations scenario, there is a "less services"
scenario which suggests that future seniors will prefer independent living (and
welcome those services that foster independence) and will resist institutionalization, preferring death (euthanasia? suicide? palliative care?) to loss of self-deter-
mination and loss of dignity. It is, of course, impossible to know whether the
person who at the age of 35 adamantly declares that he or she would prefer death
to life in a nursing home will still profess the same opinion when at 80 years of
age and faced with increasing dependency. Furthermore, regardless of what
one's preference is, reality often overrules and a person may accept a given
option even though it is not "preferred."

The Family Care versus Institutional Care Dilemma

It is often argued that families in the past were more likely to care for their
older dependent family members who either lived nearby or in a multi-genera-
tional household. Increasingly, it is argued, families are less and less able and/or
willing to care for their senior members and are therefore more and more reliant
on publicly-funded services for the care of seniors. Given small family size,
geographic mobility, and women working outside of the home, this trend might
well continue in the future. Alternatively, programs such as home care, respite
care and day care for seniors might well help the family of the future to care for
its older family members. However, the allegation that families avoid their
responsibilities to their senior members assumes that seniors are willing to be
dependent on, or want to live with, their adult offspring and that seniors are forced
against their will into public facilities. The truth is that most seniors do not want
to be dependent on, or to live with, their adult offspring. Instead, most would
voluntarily choose placement in a long-term care facility should they become
dependent rather than move in with their children (Connidis, 1983).

Attitudes in Alberta

In 1989, 1990, and again in 1991, representative samples of Albertans were
asked about their attitudes relating to issues regarding population aging. Each of
these studies formed part of the annual Alberta Survey, a public opinion poll of
adult Albertans conducted each year by the Population Research Laboratory of
the Department of Sociology at the University of Alberta. In 1989 and 1990,
these surveys were conducted by face-to-face interview in Edmonton and by

telephone interview outside of Edmonton (using a shortened version of the Edmonton questionnaire). In 1991, face-to-face interviewing was replaced with telephone surveying. In 1989, 443 Edmontonians, 370 Calgarians, and 377 other Albertans were interviewed for a total of 1190 respondents for the province as a whole. In 1990, a total of 1245 respondents were interviewed. The 1991 survey reached 1345 Albertans.

The 1989 study (Northcott, 1994 and 1990) found that three-quarters of Edmontonians believed that Canada will have problems supporting its elderly citizens in the future (this question was asked of Edmontonians only). Over half of Albertans agreed that personal taxes should be increased if the costs of supporting the elderly population rise. Half agreed that only seniors with low incomes should receive the old age security benefit, but only one-in-seven Albertans would favor reducing the value of the old age pension and other such benefits. Two-thirds of Edmontonians agreed that Canada should introduce a homemaker's pension (this question was asked of Edmontonians only). This is a program that would benefit older persons, mainly women, who have spent all or part of their married lives working in the home. When asked about other policies that might help Canada support its elderly population, only one-quarter of Albertans favored encouraging Canadians to have more children (to eventually augment the labor force), less than a quarter favored increasing immigration, and just over one-third said that Canadians should be encouraged to have their dependent elderly parents come and live with them. Finally, when asked about retirement, 69% opposed mandatory retirement (opposition to mandatory retirement is widespread throughout Canada, see Lowe, 1992). Nevertheless, the great majority of respondents planned to retire at or before the age of 65. It appears that mandatory retirement is opposed not because the individual wants to work past the age of 65, but rather because the individual wants greater flexibility of options and wants to determine for himself or herself the timing of retirement. Further analysis of these data showed that public attitudes toward these various policy alternatives were relatively consistent regardless of the sex, age, or socio-economic status of the respondent. There was no evidence of a polarization of opinion between males and females, old and young, or rich and poor.

In the 1990 Alberta Survey, respondents were told that they were to suppose that they had become old and frail and that they lived alone and could no longer care for themselves. Respondents were then asked if they would expect to move into a long-term care facility or if they would be cared for by their family or by professional care givers who would come to the respondent's home. Respondents were also asked how much they agreed or disagreed with the statement "I would prefer to die rather than become dependent on others."

Respondents to the 1990 survey were divided as to whether or not their family would care for them when they became old and frail. On the other hand, almost two in every three respondents agreed that professional care givers would come to their home to provide assistance when necessary and a similar majority agreed that they would move into a long-term care facility such as a nursing home should they become old and frail. In other words, Albertans are more likely to anticipate that in their frail old age they will rely on professional and institutional care rather than on family care. Just the same, almost half of the respondents agreed with the statement "I would prefer to die rather than become dependent on others." It appears that while many Albertans do not look forward to dependency, Albertans nevertheless would prefer to depend on professional and institutional care givers rather than on family members.

The 1991 Alberta Survey (McKinnon and Odynak, 1991) found that one-third of adult Albertans were providing support to an elderly relative. The most common type of support provided was emotional, followed by transportation, housework, financial, home maintenance, yardwork, grocery shopping, personal care, meal preparation, and banking. Of those Albertans who were employed full time and providing support to an elderly relative, 25% said that they had to take time away from paid work during the past 12 months and 20% said that they expected to change their work arrangements at some time in the future to provide eldercare. Three-quarters of adult Albertans indicated that they felt that employees should take time away from paid work to assist elderly relatives. Two-thirds said employers should make flexible work arrangements available so that their employees can provide eldercare.

Summary

In summary, attitudes towards old age might well change in the future among three groups: the general public, successive generations of seniors themselves, and the families of seniors. It seems likely that while the general public might become less agist in the future, while seniors might increasingly value their independence, and while the families of seniors might continue to assist their older family members, less favorable trends are also possible. Studies of public opinion in Alberta suggest that Albertans tend to believe that Canada will have problems supporting its senior population in the future. In such an eventuality, the majority of Albertans say that they would agree to raising taxes. Further, Albertans tend to reject encouraging higher fertility or increased immigration, or encouraging Canadians to have their dependent parents live with them as solutions to a future economic crisis. Finally, Albertans anticipate that in their frail old age they are more likely to rely on professional home care and institutional placement than on family care.

Social Ideology and the Aging of the Population

The Individualism versus Collectivism Paradox

A social ideology is a system of beliefs, values, and justifications that is widely shared. Canada's (and Alberta's) social ideology, paradoxically, is both individualistic and collectivistic in orientation (Government of Canada, 1982:138; Swartz, 1987:568), although individualism predates and tends to overshadow the more recently developed emphasis on collectivism. The ideology of individualism argues that each person is responsible for his or her own welfare or, more accurately, that each family provider is responsible for the welfare of himself or herself and for the welfare of his or her dependents (including spouse, children, sick or disabled family members, and aging parents). This ideology is tied to the so-called work ethic, which emphasizes individual effort and hard work for the purpose of providing for one's own needs and the needs of one's dependents. This emphasis on individual self-reliance (and on reliance on one's family for support) tends to be linked to a reluctance to rely on public charity.

Despite this emphasis on individualism and self-reliance, in the twentieth century Canada has experienced the emergence of the "welfare state," a collectivistic orientation that emphasizes support of the citizenry through publicly-funded state-operated programs. Canada and the provinces now have an extensive "social safety net," including hospital and medical care insurance, old age income support programs, social assistance, and unemployment insurance. In time, these programs have come to be viewed less and less as "charity" and more and more as "rights" or alternatively, as benefits that one has earned through taxes and premiums paid and through various payroll deductions.

In short, while Canadians value individual self-reliance, they also have come to rely on publicly-funded social programs. Consistent with this paradoxical blend of individualism and collectivism, current policy increasingly emphasizes public programs designed to maintain the independence of seniors. For example, home care programs provide assistance to seniors in order to help seniors remain in their own homes and apartments. It appears that there is currently an increasing emphasis being placed both on individual self-reliance and on collective caring for those in need (see chapter five).

Holistic Health Promotion Theme

Another contemporary theme is the emphasis on health promotion and illness prevention. It is increasingly argued that too much emphasis has been placed on treating illness and disability while too little emphasis has been placed on preventing health problems and on promoting health in its own right. Increasingly health is defined as complete mental, social, and physical well-being and not merely the absence of disease (see the preamble to the constitution of the World Health Organization). The Lalonde Report (1974) called for increased attention to lifestyles and living environments, in addition to the emphasis on biology and the health care delivery system. The more recent phrase "healthy public policy" (Hancock, 1982; Pederson, et al., 1988) calls for a holistic approach to health that recognizes that "health" is a function of virtually every aspect of our social and economic lives. Further to this point, the boundary between health care and social services is blurring and this is especially true for frail seniors.

The holistic health ideology contains two contradictory aspects. On the one hand, holism tends to emphasize individual responsibility for health. On the other hand, with holism there is a tendency to "medicalize" virtually every aspect of a person's life and therefore to give up some control of these diverse aspects of life to various experts.

Holism is frequently raised as a criticism of modern health care professionals who, it is said, are overly specialized and provide fragmented and illness-oriented (rather than health-oriented) care. While this criticism often leads to the argument that control over health should be wrested from the health care professional and returned to the individual, ironically, the comprehensive holistic definition of health provides a justification for intervention by a wide range of professional and technical experts and government bureaucrats, all of whom can claim to be engaged in promoting health.

Consistent with the holistic health ideology is an increasing emphasis on the quality of life in the latter years rather than an emphasis on prolongation of life, per se. This quality of life sub-theme encompasses such issues as independence, home care, avoidance/prevention of institutionalization, rehabilitation, palliative care, dying/death with dignity, living wills, and so on.

It is increasingly argued that if the "whole" needs and wishes of a heterogeneous elderly population are to be heard and acted upon, then seniors themselves must be involved at all levels of the decision-making process and given more control over funding. Such involvement would entail a shift of power from centralized to decentralized bureaucracies and from social planners, civil servants, and service providers to seniors themselves both individually and collectively. While the emphasis on empowering the individual is consistent with holistic health's emphasis on individual responsibility, nevertheless, demands for the rationalization and coordination of health care policy and service delivery tend to "empower" the bureaucracy. In other words, because of the broadening of the definition of health, an increasingly wide range of government departments, service providers, and experts are becoming involved in health care. The need to rationalize and coordinate this involvement is in tension with an emphasis on empowering the lay individual.

Summary

In summary, Canada's contemporary and emerging public ideology contains several contradictions including individual self-reliance on the one hand and reliance on the "welfare state" on the other, individual responsibility for all aspects of health versus the medicalization of many aspects of life, and individual empowerment regarding health care decisions versus the bureaucratic rationalization and coordination of policy and service delivery.

In this chapter, I have examined political, economic, attitudinal, and ideological trends and issues related to population aging. The implications of these broad societal trends for future service delivery have been discussed. The evolution of the service delivery system – past, present, and future – is examined in the following chapter.

Chapter Five
Issues in Service Delivery

In this chapter, I examine the development of programs for seniors in Canada and in Alberta with specific reference to health care and income security. The philosophical underpinnings – past, present, and future – of the service delivery system are discussed. Selected policy-oriented documents are reviewed and their recommendations for future service delivery and their underlying assumptions are examined.

The Development of Health Care Insurance Programs

This discussion focuses on the development of health insurance in Canada and in Alberta and on the evolution of health policy with specific reference to seniors. The concept of health insurance originated in Germany in the 1880s and has been debated in Canada since at least 1919 (Torrance, 1987:16; Swartz, 1987:574). Despite an ethos which stressed individual responsibility and self-reliance, and despite a free market economic ideology, the idea of health insurance appealed to many Canadians, particularly those persons who had difficulty paying for increasingly expensive health care and persons living in rural areas who were isolated from an increasingly urbanized health care delivery system (Torrance, 1987:18). The province of Saskatchewan pioneered health-insurance legislation, bringing in universal hospital insurance in 1947 and medical care insurance in 1962. Alberta initiated universal hospital insurance in 1950 (Taylor, 1987:74) and established a non-compulsory medical insurance plan in 1963 (Gelber, 1980:164; Meilicke and Storch, 1980:9) The federal government legislated national hospital insurance in 1957 and national medical care insurance in 1966 (Torrance, 1987:19-23). Alberta joined the national hospital insurance program in 1958 and the national medical-care insurance program in 1969 (Soderstrom, 1978:127).

While the 1867 British North America Act left health care as a provincial responsibility, nevertheless, the federal government used its powers of taxation to enter into cost-sharing agreements with the provinces. In regards to health insurance, the federal government required each province to meet federal standards including universal coverage (everyone was to be insured and have access to care), comprehensive coverage (a wide range of health care services were to be insured), public administration on a non-profit basis, and portability of benefits (coverage could be carried from one province to another) (Soderstrom, 1978:132-133; Chappell, et al., 1986:92).

Initially, cost-sharing between the federal and provincial governments was 50:50 (Taylor, 1980:189, 195; Taylor, 1987:83; Chappell, et al., 1986:92);

however, the financing of mental hospitals, nursing homes, homes for the aged, and other such facilities providing custodial care was excluded (Soderstrom, 1978:130, 162). Furthermore, the federal government's National Health Grants program, which began in 1948, fostered the capital construction of acute-care hospitals (Soderstrom, 1978:153, 158). In short, the post-World War II capital construction and national health insurance programs emphasized acute care rather than chronic care. Given that older people are more likely to require long-term care, seniors were disadvantaged accordingly. Health care providers and consumers alike found that there were incentives to utilize acute care even when alternative forms of care such as nursing homes, homes for the aged, or home care were more appropriate. Furthermore, the health care system itself lacked the economic incentive to develop long-term care institutions and home care programs (Soderstrom, 1978:146; Schwenger and Gross, 1980:253).

While the federal government, under the 1966 Canada Assistance Plan, began a 50:50 cost-sharing program for the poor who required care in nursing homes or homes for the aged, federal funding for the long-term care of Canadians generally did not begin until 1977 under the Extended Health Care Services Program which provided $20 per capita (increased annually per growth in the GNP) to help finance home health care and nursing home and other residential care (Soderstrom, 1978:142, 144; Taylor, 1987:86). The following year, 1978, Alberta introduced the Coordinated Home Care Program to provide both health care services and support services to Albertans living at home.

In the 1970s the federal government became concerned about the rising costs of the health insurance programs. In 1977, the Federal-Provincial Fiscal Arrangements and Established Programs Financing (EPF) Act extricated the federal government from the 50:50 cost-sharing agreement and instead tied the federal contribution to increases in the GNP (Taylor, 1987:84-86; Soderstrom, 1978:139-142). The federal government was thus protected from rapidly rising costs and the provinces gained greater flexibility and an increased incentive to control health-care spending and to implement less costly programs such as home care (Soderstrom, 1978:142-143). In 1984, the Canada Health Act consolidated the hospital insurance and medical care insurance programs (Taylor, 1987:98) and put pressure on the provinces to ban extra-billing. Alberta complied in 1986 (Northcott, 1988b:46). The 1990 federal budget further reduced federal expenditures by freezing for two years per capita EPF transfers to the provinces at 1989-90 levels and capping growth for two years (at 5% per year) in the Canada Assistance Plan payments to Ontario, British Columbia, and Alberta (Wilson, 1990:12). The 1991 federal budget extended these policies through 1994-95 (Wilson, 1991:11). The 1995 federal budget (Martin, 1995a:17-19) announced no changes in major transfers for 1995-96 and a consolidation in 1996-97 of EPF and CAP payments into a "block transfer" grant to be known as the Canada Health and Social Transfer (Martin, 1996a:10-12). Total payments would be reduced, but the provinces would have more flexibility in how they spend the grant. This program will continue the movement away from federal-provincial cost-sharing in areas of "provincial responsibility" (Martin, 1995b:12). In short, the 1990 through 1996 federal budgets put additional pressure on the provinces, and particularly on a province such as Alberta, to control health care costs.

By the early 1990s, Alberta's seniors enjoyed premium-free coverage under the Alberta Health Care Insurance Plan and a wide range of health benefits (Seniors Advisory Council for Alberta, 1991a:9-22). However, change was forthcoming (for a review and discussion of the many changes, see Engelmann, 1995; Philippon and Wasylyshyn, 1996).

In 1993, Mr. Klein was elected premier of the Province of Alberta. The province had been running budgetary deficits since the 1985-86 fiscal year. Previously, boom years in the 1970s had produced budgetary surpluses and billions of dollars had accumulated in the Alberta Heritage Saving Trust Fund, much to the envy of the other provinces. However, when Mr. Klein assumed office, he faced a string of deficits that, in total, far exceeded the value of the Heritage Fund. The government, under Klein's leadership, moved quickly. In 1994, Mr. Dinning's February 24th budget speech initiated an aggressive deficit elimination and debt reduction strategy. Government spending was to be reduced substantially in the 1994/95, 1995/96, and 1996/97 fiscal years. The deficit was to be eliminated, a goal accomplished in 1994/95 with the help of higher than expected oil and gas revenues. Surpluses were used to reduce the accumulated debt, thereby reducing debt-servicing costs (i.e., interest charges) to government.

Some felt that the cuts were too much and/or were implemented too quickly. Some felt that, instead of cutting expenditures on services, revenues should have been raised (e.g., through the introduction of a provincial sales tax). Some criticized the government as, at best, misguided, and at worst, ruthless. Others praised the government for its courage and decisiveness. Certainly, in the short term, health, education, and social security programs, including programs for seniors, experienced "pain" in the form of cutbacks, downsizing, and restructuring. Nevertheless, the long term effects of the "Klein Revolution" remain to be seen and judged. Certainly, the continued deficit-financing of social programs is not a reasonable long term strategy. Increasing debt-servicing charges take revenues away from government programs. It is ironic that the Klein government, which has been accused by some of destroying Alberta's social programs, may some day in the future be credited with saving those very same programs.

In any case, seniors benefits in Alberta have been altered in the 1990s. At the time of writing, seniors health benefits included the following (see Seniors Advisory Council for Alberta, 1995): reduction or elimination of Alberta Health Care Insurance premiums for low income seniors (under the 1994 Alberta Seniors Benefit Program), approved services provided by a physician, basic hospital services (at the standard ward level), extended health benefits (partial coverage for eyeglasses and dental services), some chiropractic services (up to specified limits), some foot care services provided by a podiatrist (up to specified limits), a yearly eye exam, physical therapy, and premium-free Alberta Blue Cross coverage [including 70% of prescription drug costs, home nursing care – such as the Victorian Order of Nurses (up to a specified limit), psychological services (up to specified limits), ambulance services, accidental dental care, appliances such as artificial limbs, and up to $100 per day for out-of-country hospital charges].

There is also an Alberta Aids to Daily Living Program (AADL), which subsidizes the costs of authorized medical equipment (e.g., hearing aids or wheelchairs) and supplies (e.g., ostomy products or incontinence supplies) for the chronically disabled or ill who are attempting to maintain their independence at home or in a home-like setting. A senior eligible for AADL benefits pays 25% of the costs to a maximum of $500 per year. Seniors with very little income are exempted from the cost-sharing requirement.

Home health care and support services are available to assist seniors who are living relatively independently in the community. Health services include case coordination, nursing, physiotherapy, occupational therapy, respiratory therapy, social work, and nutrition services. Support services include personal care assistance (e.g., bathing), and homemaking/housekeeping services. There is no charge for professional or personal care services; however, homemaking/house-keeping services cost $5 per hour up to $300 maximum per month. Seniors with very little income (e.g., eligible for the Guaranteed Income Supplement) are exempted from these charges (Seniors Advisory Council for Alberta, 1995:39).

Seniors who may require institutional continuing care are first assessed by staff from the home care program who administer the Alberta Assessment and Placement Instrument (AAPI) according to a "single point of entry" model (Seniors Advisory Council for Alberta, 1991b:82-84). When it is determined that seniors cannot be maintained at home, then admission is granted to a continuing care facility. (In Alberta, what were formerly referred to as nursing homes and auxiliary hospitals were integrated into long-term care facilities. Increasingly, these are being referred to as continuing care facilities.) As of April, 1995, charges for continuing care were $24.75 per day for standard accommodation ($26.25 per day for a room with two beds and $28.60 per day for a private room). The $24.75 per day charge is about $750 per month. The minimum monthly income for single or widowed seniors living in Alberta in July of 1995 was $955 ($392 from Old Age Security plus $466 from the Guaranteed Income Supplement and $96 from the Alberta Seniors Benefit). The 1995 rates remained unchanged in 1996.

In summary, the health care insurance system has developed in Canada as a mechanism for the collective sharing of health care costs. Hospital insurance came first, followed by medical-care insurance. An initial emphasis on acute care has been expanded to include continuing care, both facility-based (e.g., nursing homes) and community-based (e.g., home care). The principles underlying the development of these programs have been universality, accessibility, compre-hensiveness of coverage, portability, and non-profit public administration. By the late 1970s the health care insurance system was essentially in place. However, the system was costly and rapidly rising costs were coupled with increasing governmental debt and economic difficulties. During this time, emphasis has shifted from the development and expansion of the health care insurance system to the control of costs. This cost-restraint emphasis seems likely to continue well into the twenty-first century.

The Development of Income Security Programs for Seniors

The federal government's first major incursion into the social-welfare field was the 1927 Old Age Pensions Act (Chappell, 1987:490; for a discussion of the emergence of social security in Canada, see Guest, 1985). This legislation established a national, means-tested (i.e., for the poor only) old age pension for persons 70 or more years of age. This program was cost-shared between the federal and provincial governments and was provincially administered according to national standards (Chappell, 1987:490).

While the dominant ethos of the day stressed independence and individual self-sufficiency, poverty was widespread among the aged in the 1920s and the Depression of the 1930s brought the realization that individuals could become impoverished because of circumstances over which they had no control and for which they could not be held responsible (Chappell, 1987:491). Chappell implies that this enlightened perspective provided the incentive for the development of the social welfare state in which government assumed a responsibility to ensure that all Canadians have at least a subsistence income. Alternatively, it has been argued that the social welfare state developed as a strategy to pacify the working class and protect the interests of dominant elites (see, for example, Swartz, 1987). In any case, social welfare legislation proliferated, particularly after World War II. (The following chronology is taken from Statistics Canada, 1980:120-122, 124; see also Myles, 1988).

In 1951[1], the British North America Act was amended and the Old Age Security Act was implemented creating a "universal" federal old age pension for all Canadians 70 years of age and older. Also in 1951, the Old Age Assistance Act was passed which provided for a federal-provincial cost-shared income-tested pension for poor persons 65-69 years of age. Beginning in 1965, eligibility for the universal old age pension was reduced gradually to 65 years of age and in 1966[2] an income-tested guaranteed income supplement was provided for all seniors 65 and older who had insufficient income. In 1973, indexing of benefits was begun to protect seniors from inflation. In 1975, the income-tested spouse's allowance was initiated to benefit the spouses of old age pensioners providing that the couple was poor and the spouse was 60-64 years of age (after 64, the spouse would qualify for old age security and might also qualify for the guaranteed income supplement – indeed the spouse's allowance was the equivalent of these two benefits). In 1985, a widowed person's allowance was initiated to benefit low income widowed persons 60-64 years of age.

In addition to these federal programs for seniors, the province of Alberta implemented a number of its own programs for seniors. These included: reduction of property taxes (begun 1969), rental assistance grants (begun in 1972), exemption from premium payments for Alberta Health Care Insurance (begun in 1972), subsidized apartment housing (begun in 1972), the 1975 Alberta Assured Income Program which augmented the federal guaranteed income supplement for poorer seniors, income-tested grants for home repair (begun 1976), home heating rebate (begun 1982), and the 1983 Widows' Pension

Program which provides an income-tested benefit for widowed persons 55-64 years of age (Seniors Advisory Council for Alberta, 1991b:112-114).

In short, trends from 1927 to 1985 can be described as a broadening of coverage in two respects. First, coverage to the poor (as established initially by a means test and later by an income test) was extended to younger and younger age groups (from poor persons 70 or more years of age to poor persons 65 years of age and then to those poor persons 60 years of age who are either married to a person 65 or older or widowed and to poor widowed persons in Alberta 55 or older). Second, coverage under the old age pension (but not its supplements) was extended from poor persons only to all persons regardless of income and from persons over 70 years of age to persons over 65 years of age. This created two complementary programs: a universal program for all seniors 65 and older regardless of income and an income-tested program of benefits for poor seniors 65 and older (or 60-64 if married to a person 65+ or if widowed and 55-64 if widowed and living in Alberta). Income security programs had broadened significantly from 1927 when only poor seniors 70 and older received benefits.

In addition to these non-contributory programs (i.e., the beneficiaries have not previously paid directly into benefit plans), the federal Canada Pension Plan was established in 1966[3]. Both employers and employees contribute to this program and benefits depend on the amount and length of contributions (up to a maximum limit). Persons who will benefit most from the Canada Pension Plan are those who have steady, long-term, well-paid employment. Recent, older immigrants to Canada, for example, may not work long enough to establish eligibility for full benefits. While a parent has been allowed since 1983 (retro-active to 1978) to "drop out" of the labor force without penalty to care for children under 7 years of age, nevertheless, homemakers who work in the home are not covered by the Canada Pension Plan. While the possibility of a homemaker's pension has been discussed (see for example National Council of Welfare, 1984b), it does not seem likely that the Canada Pension Plan will be expanded to include homemakers in the near future.

Indeed, the days of expansion of social welfare programs may be over, at least for the time being (consider the demise of the national day care program promised in the late 1980s – see *Maclean's*, December 14, 1987). Canada has a broad "safety net" of social programs in place, and while that net could be broadened further, Canada has accumulated a huge national debt and is not in an economic position that favors the expansion of social spending. Furthermore, the demog-raphy of population aging puts increasing pressure particularly on programs that benefit seniors and on universal programs. Canada appears to have reached a critical juncture, an historical watershed (see, for example, Myles, 1988:38, 52). While social programs have been initiated and while spending on social pro-grams has increased through much of the twentieth century, the 1990s may well mark the end of this period of expansion. Indeed, under pressures to cut government spending, Canada may well be entering into a period of program contraction.

Signs of contraction are already evident: consider the 1985 attempt to partially de-index the old age security benefit, the 1989 "tax back" of that same benefit from more affluent seniors, and the elimination of the age tax credit for wealthier seniors, which was phased in from 1994 to 1995. Consider also the proposed Government of Canada Seniors Benefit, scheduled to take effect in 2001. This program will replace the existing Old Age Security and Guaranteed Income Supplements, as well as the age tax credit and the pension income tax credit, with a single benefit targeted to low- and modest-income seniors (Government of Canada, 1996; National Council of Welfare, 1996b). While it is usually politically easier for government to give rather than to take away, present and future fiscal difficulties make "giving" less likely and "taking away" more probable.

As further evidence of the transition from welfare state expansion to contraction, service reduction and restructuring have occurred in Alberta in the 1990s (Engelmann, 1995). In 1994, the property tax reduction (of up to $1000) and the renters grant (of up to $1200), which had been available to all seniors who were homeowners or renters, as well as exemption from health care premiums which had also been enjoyed by all seniors, were combined under the "targeted" Alberta Seniors Benefit Program. In other words, property tax reductions and renters grants were no longer available to financially better-off seniors. Further, financially better-off seniors were now required to pay health premiums. The Alberta Assured Income Program, which had always been targeted to lower income seniors, was also incorporated in 1994 into the Alberta Seniors Benefit Program.

Through the early to mid-1990s, other changes to Alberta's seniors benefits included the following (Engelmann, 1995): the home heating rebate was dropped, the Seniors' Emergency Medic Alert program was eliminated, a grant program for low-income seniors' home repairs was eliminated, the cost to a senior for prescription drugs under Alberta Blue Cross was increased from 20% of the cost of the medication to 30% (up to a maximum of $25 for any single prescription), extended health benefits were reduced, continuing care charges were increased, and lodge rents were "deregulated" (although they could not exceed $700 per month in 1995 and had to leave the poorest senior with at least $265 per month in disposable income, see Seniors Advisory Council for Alberta, 1995) In addition, home care support charges for better-off seniors were increased from $2 to $5 per hour (up to $300 maximum per month, depending on income), and the rents for seniors apartments were increased from 25% of the renter's income to 30% (Engelmann, 1995). In summary, following a long period of implementation and expansion of seniors benefits in Alberta, deficit reduction strategies in the 1990s ushered in a very different era. The proliferation and expansion of programs gave way to program cuts.

The Philosophical Underpinnings of the Income-Security and Health-Care Programs

Canada and Alberta have long had an ethos which has placed a heavy emphasis on individual self-reliance. Early in this country's history, the poor, sick, and aged were left to themselves, to their families, and to charitable social organizations (such as churches). Formal government initiatives were minimal. Nevertheless, in the twentieth century, and especially since World War II, federal, provincial, and municipal governments have become increasingly involved in the provision of services to the poor, sick, and aged.

Canada's social services have been established on the basis of several different principles. In the area of health care, the principle of universality has played a central role. That is, health care is available to anyone with medical need; there is no means or income testing. Universal programs avoid the stigma of being seen as "charity" and avoid the logistics and costs of establishing eligibility. Nevertheless, Canada also has income-tested social programs and contributory programs (see Neysmith, 1987, and Chappell, et al., 1986:95-97 for discussions of these options). The guaranteed income supplement, for example, is an income-tested program for seniors and the Canada Pension Plan provides a retirement pension for older retired employees who have established eligibility through "contributions" paid into the plan.

Contemporary Canadian society paradoxically maintains both its historical emphasis on individual self-reliance on the one hand, and, on the other hand, a more recent but strong commitment to social programs such as medicare and old age security. Furthermore, Canada has both universal and selected (income-tested) programs, both age-based and non-age-based programs, and both contributory and non-contributory programs. Table 5.1 illustrates these various program options. The question is, what will be the philosophical underpinnings of Canada's future service delivery system? Will these various divergent and often contradictory themes continue together or will one or several themes receive increasing emphasis at the expense of the others?

Table 5.1

A Typology Illustrating the Various Bases of Canada's Health Insurance
and Income Security Programs

	Based on Age	
Basis	Yes	No
Universal	e.g., Old Age Security (until 1989)	e.g., Health Insurance
Income- or Means-Tested	e.g., Guaranteed Income Supplement; Old Age Security (from 1989)	e.g., Social Assistance
Contributory	e.g., Canada Pension Plan	e.g., Unemployment Insurance

In the future, age-based programs may come increasingly under attack. Age is a social category similar to sex or race (Neysmith, 1987:587). Programs that benefit one sex and not another, or one race and not another, are increasingly unacceptable. Similarly, age by itself may become increasingly unacceptable as a criterion for social entitlement. Furthermore, in times of economic constraint, the principle of universality has come increasingly under attack. As Neysmith (1987:591-592) points out, a universal program such as old age security has an image problem in times of economic constraint in that there is a highly visible distribution of resources (e.g., an OAS cheque mailed monthly to all seniors regardless of need) and a rather invisible and not always equitable recovery of these resources through the mechanism of taxation[4].

"Need" (as established through means- or income-testing) and "merit" (as established through contributions) are being increasingly emphasized over universality as bases for social entitlement, although Neysmith (1987:594) argues that need and merit claims are quite different. For example, the pension system is likely to continue to be based on merit (e.g., past contributions, number of years worked, levels of income) reflecting our society's ideals of individualism, freedom of choice, personal responsibility, and reward for initiative and success. Such a system may be justified by reference to the ideal of equality of opportunity, but such a system leads to inequality of outcome. For those persons who are disadvantaged in the outcome, programs based on need will continue to provide a "safety net."

In summary, assuming that economic constraint will be a factor over the next decade or so, and assuming that economic policy will have important implications for social policy (Neysmith, 1987:594), it seems likely that there will be a shift in emphasis away from universal programs to programs based on need. Furthermore, age, by itself, (i.e., universal age-based programming) is likely to become less salient as a criterion for social entitlement. An emphasis on individual responsibility and self-sufficiency is likely to continue and may indeed receive increased attention. Consider the contemporary rhetoric which emphasizes independence for seniors, individual empowerment, health promotion and illness prevention, self care, informal care, home care, RRSPs, and so on. The emerging rhetoric resounds with the ideals of individualism and self-reliance and has the added and timely appeal of promising reduced expenditures. At the same time, society's collective responsibility in the future is likely to be defined on the basis of need, i.e., the provision of a social "safety net" with benefits offered primarily to the needy. These programs will continue to benefit those seniors who become poor or sick or too frail to live independently.

A Review of Selected Policy-Oriented Documents

The WHO Definition of Health

The 1946 Constitution of the World Health Organization defined health as complete physical, mental, and social well-being and more than the absence of disease. This definition argues that health is different from illness and can be pursued in its own right. Further, this definition argues that health is more than biology and that the physical and mental aspects of health are interrelated with the social and economic. This conceptualization of health is broad and idealistic; indeed, everything appears to be health-related. It can be argued that this conceptualization is so broad that it is useless, and so idealistic that it is impractical. On the other hand, this definition has been quoted and referenced frequently for decades. Perhaps its staying power derives from the recognition that the health of the individual is tied to the health of the collective and that the biological, psychological, economic, social, and political realms are interdependent. The 1946 WHO definition reflects a systems perspective, an ecological perspective, a holistic perspective, and a proactive (and not merely reactive) perspective. These perspectives have been gaining in popularity – consider the increased emphasis on health promotion, the emerging environmental health movement, and the turning of the old phrase "public health policy" into the phrase "healthy public policy" (see Pederson, et al., 1988). The WHO's enduring conceptualization of health enjoys a particular saliency in regards to the well-being of seniors, particularly frail seniors for whom medical and social needs often blur and overlap and for whom issues of income, housing, social support, and so on are often as important as the provision of health care itself.

The Lalonde Report: A New Perspective

In 1974, the federal government published a document titled *A New Perspective on the Health of Canadians* under the signature of Marc Lalonde, then Minister of National Health and Welfare. In this book, mortality data were analyzed by age, sex, and cause. It was argued that a great many deaths in Canada were "premature" as a result of unhealthy lifestyles and environments. Further, it was argued that while the great bulk of health expenditures went to biological research and to the health care delivery system, it was time to shift some dollars away from these areas and into the promotion of healthier lifestyles and environments. This document was very influential and played an important role in focusing attention on the issues of health promotion and illness prevention. Critics nevertheless suggested that this report individualized health issues and ran the risk of "blaming the victim." Smoking, for example, was identified by the Lalonde Report as a major cause of premature mortality. The Lalonde Report implied that more dollars be spent trying to persuade individuals not to smoke. The critics argued that the report seemed to ignore the social and economic context in which smoking occurs. In other words, the critics argued that the Lalonde Report placed the responsibility for health on the individual rather than on society.

Achieving Health for All

In 1986, Jake Epp, then Minister of National Health and Welfare, published *Achieving Health For All: A Framework for Health Promotion*. This document takes a broad definition of health reflecting the WHO definition ("complete physical, mental, and social well-being") and echoes Lalonde's 1974 statement by proposing a "health promotion" approach. Further, this document argues that Canada's present health care system fails to deal adequately with contemporary issues including reducing inequities in health between low- and high-income groups, preventing health problems, and helping people cope with chronic conditions, disabilities, and mental health problems. As a means of dealing with these issues, a health promotion strategy is proposed. This strategy has both an individual and a collective emphasis. For example, consider the definition of "health promotion" used in this document (taken from the World Health Organization): "the process of enabling people to increase control over, and to improve, their health" and, further, "a mediating strategy between people and their environments, synthesizing personal choice and social responsibility . . ." (Epp, 1986:6).

The proposed health promotion framework contains three health promotion mechanisms: self-care, mutual aid (including support from family, neighborhood, voluntary organizations, and/or self-help groups), and healthy physical, social, and economic environments (whether at home, school, or work). The proposed health promotion framework also contains three implementation strategies including fostering public participation, strengthening community health services, and coordinating healthy public policy. The document concludes with two observations. First, it is recognized that "we cannot invite people to assume responsibility for their health and then . . . fault them for illnesses and disabilities which are the outcome of wider social and economic circumstances" (p. 12). Second, it is noted that, in a time of economic scarcity, "The pressures created by an aging population and the growing incidence of disabilities in our society will take a heavy toll on our financial resources" (pp. 12-13). However, it is argued that "the health promotion approach has the potential over the long term to slow the growth in health care costs" (p. 13). In other words, the federal government's health promotion strategy seems to be simultaneously an attempt to deal with some of the pressing health issues of the day and at the same time reduce costs by shifting emphasis from expensive treatment to prevention and from the expensive formal health care delivery system to the informal support system with its focus on self-care and on family and volunteer supports.

Aging: Shifting the Emphasis

In 1986, Health and Welfare Canada released a working paper titled *Aging: Shifting the Emphasis*. In this document, it is argued explicitly that the emphasis in health care for seniors must be shifted from expensive hospital-based acute care and long-term institutional care to community-based services, with the intent of helping seniors to live independently in the community. It is noted that "This is what [seniors] want and this is what seems to be the most economical" (p. 10).

Moving Into the Future: For the Health of Albertans

These same themes appear in a document released by Jim Dinning, then Minister of Alberta Community and Occupational Health (Alberta Community and Occupational Health, n.d.) about the same time as Epp's 1986 federal statement. This document notes that lifestyles and living environments are important determinants of health and that chronic problems have replaced infectious diseases as the major source of illness and disability. This document argues that increased emphasis must be placed on health promotion, illness prevention, and community care, that is, the care and support of individuals in their own homes and communities. It is noted that not only does community care promote social and mental well-being, "In addition, it can be an effective and economical alternative to institutional care" (p. 3). Further, "community care will allow treatment of disease and disability in a way that advances the quality of care while helping to manage costs" (p. 8). Once again it is argued that changes in emphasis proposed for the health care system will result not only in better care, but will also result in less expensive care.

Caring and Responsibility

These same themes are again explicit in the statement of social policy released by the Government of Alberta in 1988. This statement was designed to guide social policy for Alberta through the 1990s and into the next century. This document describes Albertans as "enterprising individuals," proud of "our independence, our initiative, and our commitment . . ." (p. 2). Albertans are also described as a compassionate and caring people who "have worked together, and supported and cared for each other, especially during times of adversity" (p. 4). Alberta's diverse social programs are cited as evidence of this compassion and caring. It is argued, however, that Alberta's social policy does not simply reflect ideals of individual self-reliance on the one hand and compassion for the less fortunate on the other. Rather, economic and social factors are "not only related but inseparable" (p. 1) and while "Albertans have tended to regard social policy as being separate from economic policy[, t]here must be a consistency between social and economic policies" (p. 2). In other words, a healthy economy can provide the means and opportunity to create and expand social programs and, vice versa, social programs can develop human resources and foster individual self-reliance and initiative and thereby benefit the economy (p. 1). More to the point, in the past Alberta's booming economy, especially in the 1974-1983 period (pp. 2, 5), facilitated the establishment and expansion of many social programs. The mid-1980s downturn of Alberta's economy (p. 3) has brought "adverse economic times" (p. 1) and an "awareness of the need to review and update . . . social policies . . . and . . . to set a clear direction for the future" (p. 3; see also p. 6).

In short, this document emphasizes two themes: individual self-reliance and social programs to support persons in need. Further, this document argues that in times of economic affluence, social programs can be expanded, but in times of fiscal restraint it is necessary to re-emphasize individual self-reliance. These themes of individual and collective responsibility are always in a dynamic tension and one theme tends to compromise the other. That is, an over-emphasis on self-reliance tends to result in inadequate social programming, while an overemphasis on social programming can destroy individual initiative. Despite this tension between these two somewhat contradictory themes, Alberta has tended to pursue both simultaneously, attempting to maintain a balance between individual and collective responsibility. This balance, however, is influenced by economics. A healthy economy allows the balance to shift in the direction of social programming; a weaker economy tends to shift the balance in the direction of individual (and family, community, etc.) self-reliance. Accordingly, in a time of fiscal constraint, the Government of Alberta has developed a statement of social policy that "reflects a philosophy that stresses individual initiative, independence, and responsibility" and "which is built on a firm foundation of strong and enterprising citizens who are prepared to accept challenges, take decisive actions, and accept responsibility for their actions" (p. 9). The statement of social policy reads as follows:

The Government of Alberta recognizes that social and economic development are inseparable. It is committed to building on our tradition of caring for each other. . . .

The government will provide the necessary leadership and overall responsibility for provincial social policies, and will provide support and resources to create an environment in which Albertans can work together, be self-reliant, and take responsibility for their own lives, their families, and their communities.

Government policies and programs will be designed to promote cooperative and independent initiatives of individual Albertans while at the same time ensuring that those who, for a variety of reasons, must depend on social programs for support are able to live dignified and meaningful lives. (p. 9)

A New Vision for Long Term Care

Also in 1988, the Committee on Long Term Care for Senior Citizens, chaired by Dianne Mirosh, MLA, released a discussion paper on long-term care in Alberta. This review was initiated because of concerns stemming from the aging of the population, the "high consumption of health care services among the elderly," the "increasing cost of institutional care," and the constraints of finite resources (p. 1). This paper is an attempt to assess demographic, social, and health care trends over the next two decades and their impact on Alberta's long-term care system (p. 2). The committee argued that a new perspective is required to take into account the increasing numbers of seniors, their changing needs and preferences, and the need for future service delivery to be "cost effective" (p. 9). The committee recommended that the "new vision" for long-term care should attempt to "Foster and promote a continuum of appropriate long-term care for the aging population, emphasizing independence and quality of life in a community and family-based environment, commensurate with the resources of the province and the individual" (p. 9).

Several directions for change were recommended including: single point of entry to long-term care, health promotion, increased voluntary support, expansion of community-based services, emphasis on seniors' independence, development of housing alternatives for seniors, merging of nursing homes and auxiliary hospitals into long-term care centres, improved training for providers of care, and improved coordination of the long-term care system. A number of these recommendations were specifically justified as cost-limiting mechanisms. For example, single point of entry was promoted to forestall inappropriate utilization of facility-based services by emphasizing community-based services, thereby ensuring "appropriate use of services as a means of controlling costs in the system" (p. 12). Encouraging volunteer activities also implies cost-savings,

particularly where volunteer supports help prevent or forestall expensive institutionalization. Similarly, community-based services and an emphasis on
seniors' independence were advocated to prevent or forestall institutionalization
and thereby reduce costs.

The expenses involved in nursing home and auxiliary hospital construction
and operation are discussed in this report and it is concluded that "In light of the
expected increase in the number of elderly, clearly we can no longer afford to
build beds at the same rate as we have done in the past" (p. 41). They also argue
that long-term patients in the acute-care hospital should be moved as soon as
possible to less expensive modes of care, while those remaining in the acute-care
hospital more than 60 days should be assessed accommodation charges (pp.
43-45). In summary, this report recommends changes designed not only to
improve care but also to reduce the overall cost of care.

Home Care in Alberta: New Directions in Community Support

This document was released in 1992 by Alberta Health to generate discussion
about the future role of Home Care in Alberta in the face of health system reform.
The Coordinated Home Care Program had begun in 1978. It was expanded in
1984 to provide support services to seniors regardless of their need for health
services. In 1990, Single Point of Entry (SPE) was implemented province-wide
for persons requiring long-term care in order to ensure that all possible community options are explored "before admission to a long term care facility is
considered" (p. 6).

The authors of this document stress the role of home care in reducing the
health care costs of an aging population. Consider the following excerpts:

It is also clear that Home Care plays a major role in easing pressures in
the health system. As the health system undergoes reform, Home Care will
be expected to assume new and increasingly important roles. (p. iii)

The Home Care Program will continue to grow and expand in the future.
The program's broad mission is to "assist Albertans to achieve and maintain health, well-being, and personal independence in their homes." (p. 1)

The authors observe that the increased emphasis on home care will be driven
in part by population aging and fiscal constraints (pp. 2-4). Clearly, government
is concerned about the cost implications of an increasing number of seniors,
especially in the context of fiscal difficulties. Institutional care is very expensive.
By restricting long-term continuing institutional care to those most in need,
dollars can be saved. This is to be accomplished by relying increasingly on
continuing care being provided in the community, primarily in seniors' homes.
Accordingly, the importance of self-care, informal support, and the involvement
of volunteers is noted (pp. 20-21).

Of course, home care also involves formal supports, that is, paid professionals
serving seniors in their homes. The shift from nursing home to client's home,
and the shift from continuous professional care to professional care, as needed,
supplemented by unpaid labor (usually from spouse or other family members),
is expected to reduce overall costs. Further, surveys indicate that generally both

seniors and their family caregivers would welcome home care to prevent or forestall institutionalization.

Budget '94: Securing Alberta's Future

Following the provincial election in 1993, the Alberta government launched an attack on the budget deficit (Dinning, 1994). The government planned to eliminate the deficit in four years through deep cuts in expenditures (rather than through increasing taxes). The Deficit Elimination Act was passed by the legislature in May of 1993. The 1994 budget reaffirmed the deficit elimination strategy, and announced that health services would be fundamentally restructured, community-based health programs would be expanded, and a new seniors benefit program would be implemented.

Regarding the new seniors benefit, the 1994 budget stated:

During the past two years [1992 and 1993], the province has consulted with seniors on programs providing benefits to them. . . . a new program, the Alberta Seniors Benefit, has been designed. This program is based on the following principles: fairness, protection of lower income seniors, benefits based on income, one-window access, and ongoing monitoring and consultation. The new program will consolidate five [in the end, four] existing programs into a single benefit for seniors. . . . seniors whose incomes exceed the prescribed level will not receive any benefits under the new program. (p. 33; see also p. 75)

The health care delivery system will be restructured. . . . Both the number of acute care beds and annual hospital treatment days per 1000 population will be reduced. A portion of the savings will be reallocated to enhance community-based services that will allow Albertans to remain in their own homes. . . . Senior citizens will have access to universal services and benefits on a comparable basis to other Albertans and would pay Health Care Insurance premiums. Lower income seniors would have all or a portion of those premiums paid on their behalf through the proposed Alberta Seniors Benefit. (pp. 92-93)

In short, the Alberta Government announced the end of age-based universal benefits available only to seniors. That is, programs that benefitted all seniors, regardless of income, were eliminated, including property tax reduction and waiver of health care premiums. Universal programs, such as medicare, that benefitted seniors and non-seniors alike, were retained. Seniors in Alberta would henceforth be treated like all other Albertans.

Less financially well-off seniors would qualify for a Seniors Benefit. Note that income-testing coupled with age, not age alone, defines entitlement. There is a clear movement away from universal entitlement towards entitlement based on need. In other words, those who are able to pay their own way will be required to do so. Those who cannot pay will receive assistance.

The government might well expect that future seniors will be increasingly independent. With more and more seniors qualifying for the Canada Pension, and further, with more women working in the labor force and earning private pensions, in the future there will be more "double-pensioner" retired families (Poulin, 1996). Even after the death of the spouse, fewer widows than today will be poor as more widows will have their own pensions. In short, by eliminating universal benefits to seniors, future costs are restricted to only those seniors in need. Given that most seniors most of the time are not in need, and given that future seniors may be better off than present seniors, one can see how government hopes to reduce the costs of an aging population.

In order to justify spending cuts to seniors programs, the 1994 budget argued that current fiscal difficulties constitute a "spending problem, not a revenue problem" (p. 110). Further, the budget statement pointed out that governmental deficits mean rising debt loads and increasing interest costs. Money paid by government as interest on the debt means less money "is available to fund programs or to put back into taxpayers' pockets" (p. 39).

The 1994 budget pointed to other problems attached to deficit financing.

Deficits absorb savings, cause interest rates to rise and crowd out private investment [slowing or reversing the growth in national prosperity] . . . Deficits transfer costs to future generations – taxing future generations to pay for today's consumption. Each generation of taxpayers should pay for the government services they consume. Only by paying full price for government services, can the public properly determine what level of services it wants governments to provide. Persistent high deficits are only delayed expenditure cuts or future tax increases. (p. 109)

In other words, it was argued that equity among the generations is a central issue. It was argued that services to seniors that cost more today than the government can afford, without borrowing, are unjustified because they burden future generations. These future generations will be required to pay for the services that their parents and grandparents received, with no necessary guarantee that the same benefits will be available to them when their time comes. In short, the argument that future practices are not fair to future generations was made as a justification for cuts in present program spending.

Healthy Albertans Living in a Healthy Alberta: A Three-Year Business Plan

In the same year as the Budget '94 statement, Alberta Health (1994b) released its three-year business plan for 1994/95 through 1996/97. (See also Alberta Health's 1995 business plan for the years 1995/96 through 1997/98 as well as the Alberta Health Planning Secretariat's 1993 document titled *Starting Points*.) The business plan noted the increasing numbers and proportion of seniors and the increase in disabilities and chronic conditions as people age. Further, the business plan observed that the current fiscal situation required that health care be restructured to provide less costly care. In short, the issues of population aging and fiscal difficulties were again raised as justification for cost-saving reforms.

Alberta Health's 1994 business plan reiterated familiar themes: shifting from illness care to prevention of illness, keeping Albertans healthy and independent as long as possible in their own homes, promoting individual responsibility for health, encouraging independence, and assisting Albertans with health limitations to stay in their own homes and communities (pp. 3-5). A less familiar theme also appeared. There was mention of a "growing concern about the quality of life in the final days until death" coupled with the suggestion that, for some conditions, a quality of life orientation (such as palliative care) "is more appropriate than an emphasis on cure" (pp 3-4).

These phrases indirectly refer to the high cost of dying and suggest that there are cheaper ways to care for those who are near death's door. Aggressive attempts to prolong life (that is, to extend the "quantity" of life) tend to be very expensive. Furthermore, attempts to prolong the life of the dying are associated with extremely negative images. Consider the stereotype of the person dying in the intensive care unit, kept alive against his/her will, without control, without dignity, while strangers aggressively and futilely push high technology into every orifice of the person's body. In the face of such stereotypes, reference to the "quality of life" has an obvious appeal. Perhaps less obvious are the anticipated cost savings. Palliative care, which focuses on managing symptoms to promote quality of life rather than on seeking cures to prolong life, has a double-barrelled appeal. Like home care, palliative care promises that you can have the service you prefer and it will cost less! That is, staying in your own home as long as possible, and having as good a quality of life as possible, are both popular themes and have the added advantage of promising cost savings.

Will people actually get preferred services for less dollars? Perhaps . . . if home care is able to adequately meet peoples' needs and if palliative care is able to adequately serve those who are truly dying. There is a risk that home care will be inadequate to meet the needs of at least some seniors, while at the same time denying these seniors access to more costly institutional care. Further, there is a risk that persons who might benefit from costly curative care will be denied that care and, instead, will be kindly, and more cheaply, palliated into the hereafter. The ideals of home care, quality of life, palliative care, and the efficient use of limited economic resources have merit. However, the goodness of an idea is no guarantee that the idea will be well used. The movement toward home care and palliative care for the dying should be monitored with a hopeful, but careful, eye.

Alberta Health's 1994 business plan also emphasized that entitlement to health services will be "subject to what society can afford" and that "access will be based on need, not age" (p. 5). Further, the plan stated that "seniors will have access to universal services and benefits on the same basis as other Albertans" (p. 13). Seniors would be required to pay health care premiums and other charges "based on ability to pay" (p. 7). In short, the end of universal age-based health benefits was announced. Consistent with the 1994 provincial budget plan, benefits would no longer go to all seniors, but instead would be directed only to lower income seniors.

Government of Alberta Strategic Business Plan for Alberta Seniors 1996/97 to 1998/99

This document (Government of Alberta, 1996) was included in the Alberta Community Development Business Plan for 1996/97 through 1998/99. (Recall that since 1993, seniors' issues in Alberta were the responsibility of the Department of Community Development.) The government's strategic plan noted the increasing number and proportion of seniors. Many of the strategies proposed in the plan were designed to control the costs of programs for seniors.

The government's mission statement regarding seniors was stated as follows: "To enhance opportunities for Alberta seniors to improve their health, independence, and well-being." To accomplish this mission, three goals were stated:

To encourage the development of service options that promote individual responsibility and independence;

To promote a range of service options that support and protect those who need assistance; and

To provide services that are affordable, sustainable, and achieve intended and measurable results. (p. 25)

In order to accomplish each of these goals, a series of strategies were laid out (pp. 25-29). These include shifting governmental funds from institutional care to community care, preventing inappropriate institutionalization, encouraging people to become self-reliant and responsible for their own care, ensuring that the most vulnerable seniors are protected, assisting lower income seniors through the income-tested Alberta Seniors Benefit program, charging seniors for some services depending on their ability to pay, designing services for seniors to be more affordable for both taxpayers and seniors, and integrating services to create greater efficiencies, lower costs, and higher quality.

In short, the Alberta Government's plan for seniors is motivated by two factors: first, the increasing number and proportion of seniors in the population, and second, a desire to control the costs of providing services to this growing segment of the population. The goal of controlling costs is to be accomplished in two ways: first, by reducing expensive institutionally-based services while expanding less expensive community-based services, and second, by requiring those who can be independent or who can pay for services to do so while continuing to provide services for those persons who cannot. This overall strategy is intended not only to reduce current expenditures for seniors, but also to reduce the rate of growth in future expenditures for seniors. Seniors will no longer be entitled to benefits simply because they are seniors. Instead, programs will be targeted only to those seniors who are in need. Government will no longer have to be concerned with the growing number of seniors generally, although government will remain concerned with the growing number of needy seniors. Given that most seniors, most of the time, are not in need, the number of needy seniors will be far less than the number of seniors in total. The shift in focus from seniors in general to needy seniors, coupled with the provision of less costly services to needy seniors, is intended to reduce the future costs of supporting the aging population.

The Seniors Benefit: Securing the Future

In 1996, the Federal Government announced its intention to implement a new Seniors Benefit program beginning in the year 2001 (Government of Canada, 1996; Martin, 1996a:13-14; Martin, 1996b). It was proposed that this benefit would replace the existing Old Age Security and Guaranteed Income Supplement programs. The Seniors Benefit would also replace the age and pension income tax credits.

The Seniors Benefit is to be income-tested and fully indexed to inflation. Most seniors will be as well off or better off under the new Seniors Benefit than they are under the current system. Benefits will be tax free and mailed monthly.

It was argued that the new Seniors Benefit is required because Canada's retirement income system "faces a challenge from the ageing of our population .... [T]he cost of our public pension programs [will increase] faster than our capacity to pay for them .... [and] Canadians ... are concerned about the future sustainability of the retirement income system" (Government of Canada, 1996:13).

The Seniors Benefit promises cost savings through better targeting of benefits to lower-income seniors and reducing or eliminating assistance to those with higher incomes. Further, targeting benefits to lower and modest income seniors will slow the rate of growth in program costs. Finally, it is expected that the average income of seniors will "grow faster than the rate of inflation in the coming decades." This would mean that over time relatively fewer seniors would require full or even partial benefits (Government of Canada, 1996:14, 25, 33, 35; Martin, 1996a:13).

It appears that "sustainability" has become a key word. In a section titled "The Sustainability Problem," it is stated: "The future affordability of our public pension programs is challenged by major demographic and economic changes. ... These challenges must be addressed to ensure that the programs will be preserved for tomorrow's seniors" (Government of Canada, 1996:23).

The specific demographic changes that were discussed include: increased life expectancy, which means that seniors tend to collect benefits for a longer period of time than in the past; the baby boom generation, which will begin a seniors boom starting in 2011; and the baby bust generation, which follows the aging boomers. The seniors boom indicates an increasing number of retirees while the baby bust implies a relative decline in the number of persons in the labor force paying taxes to support the aging population. In other words, the "old age labor force dependency ratio" is expected to become less favorable, with seniors becoming an increasing "burden" for taxpayers.

Anticipated economic changes include "slower growth in productivity and wage levels," the increasing costs of public pensions, and "the pressures of an ageing population on health and social services costs." While slower economic growth may or may not be the case in the future, it is argued that "It would simply not be responsible to count on a return to the high wage growth or high labor force growth of the 1960s and 1970s" (Government of Canada, 1996:24).

The proposed federal Seniors Benefit is justified on the basis of population aging and increasing costs. The government argues that today's programs are not sustainable, meaning that they are not economically viable over the long term. This raises questions of generational equity. It is argued that changes are necessary if retirement income security is to be preserved in a manner that is fair to both present and future generations of seniors. In the words of the Government of Canada's *Securing the Future* statement:

> In the end, these challenges come down to two questions:
> Will young Canadians be willing and able to support the public pension system?
> Will the programs be there for today's youth when they retire?
> It is crucial that we take action now to make our public pensions sustainable and affordable. (p. 25)

Conclusion

Service delivery for seniors in the future will be influenced by several concurrent trends. First of all, the population aging trend implies increasing demand for services and therefore increasing costs. Second, trends in service costs are more than a simple reflection of demographic trends. Costs also reflect the types and amounts of services provided and the charges levied for those services. With respect to health care services, for example, increasing numbers (per capita) of medical practitioners, increasing (per capita) utilization of services, new and expensive technologies, and inflation of physicians' fees, nurses' salaries, medical supplies, etc., all imply increasing costs (Barer, et al., 1986 and 1987; Culyer, 1988:30-33; Roos, Shapiro, and Roos, 1987:338-342; Evans, 1987a:167, 175-176; Evans, 1987b; Evans, 1989). Third, a less than booming economy, annual budget deficits, a large accumulated debt, and high debt servicing costs imply a restricted ability to pay. All of these trends in combination explain the emerging directions in services for seniors.

Emerging service delivery themes include: a focus on community-based services, coordination of services, promotion of health and well-being, targeting of services to those most in need, restructuring of programs in the context of fiscal constraint, sustainability, and generational equity. The focus on community-based services involves a shift away from facility-based care to community-based care, an increased emphasis on independence, self-reliance, self-care, family support, informal community supports, volunteerism, and formal home care and support services. Generally, care is cheaper if provided outside of a facility and, of course, is cheaper if you can utilize unpaid caregivers.

The emphasis on the coordination of services involves centralized assessment and placement mechanisms (e.g., single point of entry) to coordinate the delivery of a wide range of services (e.g., the continuum of care and the social safety net) so as to maximize independence and minimize costs by assigning the "lowest" level of care appropriate. Illness prevention and the promotion of health and well-being are also intended to reduce the need for expensive care.

The targeting of programs to lower-income seniors indicates the end of age-based programming. That is, programs such as Old Age Security that benefit all seniors regardless of need are being replaced with programs for needy seniors only. The anticipated increase in the numbers and proportion of seniors in the population raises concerns that programs that benefit all seniors will become too costly. Eliminating higher-income seniors from coverage will help to reduce costs.

Targeting is part of a fundamental restructuring of health and social programs that has been motivated by the demographic trend towards an aging population in the context of fiscal difficulties. Federal and provincial governments have struggled with budgetary deficits, mounting debt-loads, and resulting interest charges. Deficit reduction/elimination has become the order of the day. While raising taxes and stimulating the economy could help, the preferred strategy seems to be the restructuring of social programs in order to reduce both present and future government spending.

Justification for these various cost-saving strategies tends to centre around the issues of sustainability and generational equity. It is argued that present programs for seniors are not sustainable and will become increasingly unaffordable. Accordingly, it is suggested that substantial change is required if programs for seniors are to continue to be available in the future. Further, it is argued that substantial change is necessary in the interests of "fairness" and "equity." It is pointed out that costly programs that benefit one generation at the expense of another are inequitable. Programs that prove to be unsustainable will benefit the older generation, cost the younger generation, and then collapse before the younger generation has its turn to benefit. Further, programs that are presently unaffordable contribute to deficits which are covered by governmental borrowing. The resulting debt becomes an obligation inherited by the younger generation. In short, the younger generation ends up paying for yesterday's, today's, and tomorrow's seniors and paying far more than it will ever receive in turn.

It appears that there is a perception that little can be done about the aging trend itself and also that fiscal restraint will be a long-term condition. Accordingly, both the Federal Government and the Alberta Government have signaled their intent to reduce present and future service and benefit costs.

Chapter Six
Rhetoric and Reality

In the previous five chapters I have examined the phenomenon of population aging in Alberta. This final chapter is a review and discussion focusing on the "facts" of population aging and the various interpretations that are placed on this phenomenon, particularly with respect to implications for the future. An attempt is made to distinguish rhetoric from reality.

The term "rhetoric" refers to language that is used to persuade or influence. For the purposes of this present discussion, the term will refer to language which is designed to place a particular interpretation upon some aspect of population aging. While the goal of this chapter is to distinguish rhetoric and reality, nevertheless, it is virtually impossible to separate these two dimensions completely, especially when speculating about the future. Furthermore, "reality" is understood only through processes of perception and interpretation, which in turn are influenced by cultural frames of reference and by social dynamics, which give rise to a collective definition of the situation. In other words, reality is given "meaning" through a process of social construction. In short, reality and rhetoric are inherently intertwined; nevertheless, rhetoric can be challenged and scrutinized, and underlying assumptions, veiled motivations, and implications can be laid bare.

In chapter one, I argued that while population aging might seem to be primarily a demographic trend, nevertheless, understanding a society's reaction to this phenomenon requires a focus on much more than demography. In particular, I argued that an emphasis on politics and economics is required. I further argued in chapter one that rhetoric and ideology tend to emerge to place a definition upon a phenomenon such as population aging, a definition which tends to serve selected political and economic interest groups and agendas. In short, the apocalyptic definitions of population aging as a "crisis" or "challenge" or "problem" may or may not fit the facts and may constitute a manipulative social construction of reality. The following is an examination of the political economy of aging in Alberta and the social construction of the population aging "problem."

The Political Economy of Aging in Alberta

Alberta has a relatively low percentage of seniors in its population in comparison to other Canadian provinces and in comparison to many of the developed countries of the world. Furthermore, the aging of the population trend in Alberta will unfold slowly over the next three or four decades. Alberta's projected percentage of seniors for 2016 is in the 13-15% range, levels already exceeded without crisis in a number of European countries, in the state of Florida, and in the city of Victoria, for example. Furthermore, this expected percentage of seniors is already equalled in the western provinces of Saskatchewan, Manitoba, and British Columbia. Additionally, the percentage of persons 85 years of age and older in Alberta (those seniors most likely to require public assistance) is projected to increase from 1.0% to around 1.8% by the year 2016. While this statistic is just short of "doubling," it is nevertheless only a small increase from 1 person per 100 to less than 2 persons per 100.

So why all the fuss over the aging of the population in Alberta? Various government documents, pronouncements, and policy changes suggest that Alberta faces a serious population aging problem that should not and cannot be ignored. This view of population trends has been labelled "apocalyptic demography" (Robertson, 1991) and "demographic determinism" (Marshall, 1994). The media have also played an important role in disseminating and propagating this crisis scenario. Furthermore, public opinion data indicate that the general public in Alberta has been greatly influenced by this rhetoric and does believe that there is or will be a population aging crisis (Northcott, 1994). Does this perception of crisis, shared by government and public alike, fit the facts? It is not at all clear that the demographic data for Alberta justify, either now or in the future, the perception of a "crisis."

Indeed, I will argue that the "problem" is not the future aging of the Alberta population. Rather, the problem is that Alberta's economy went into recession in 1982 and struggled for a decade. Consequently, the Province of Alberta ran a string of budgetary deficits from 1985/86 to 1993/94 and accumulated a substantial debt. Furthermore, Alberta has not been unique economically. Indeed, the fiscal difficulties experienced in Alberta have occurred elsewhere in Canada, in the United States, in European countries such as Britain and France, and in Australia. As these various governments have sought to come to grips with expenditures that far out-strip revenues, it has been easy to blame the aging of the population for fiscal difficulties and to attempt to cut back programs for seniors. The resulting policy discussions in various parts of the developed world and the accompanying rhetoric provide the context in which Alberta has interpreted and responded to its fiscal dilemmas and population aging trend.

In short, the population aging crisis has been socially constructed largely outside of Alberta. Alberta's population is relatively youthful and is aging relatively slowly. The use of the crisis definition in Alberta has more to do with fiscal difficulties than with population aging, per se.

Given that expenditures on seniors in contemporary welfare states such as Canada and the province of Alberta make up a very significant portion of governmental budgets, it is understandable that governments facing fiscal restraint would attempt to reduce spending on seniors' programs. What is curious is the tendency to "blame the victim." While it is true that seniors are major beneficiaries of governmental programs, and while it is true that population aging may make a bad situation worse, nevertheless, in Alberta, it cannot be argued that population aging **caused** the economic difficulties of the 1980s and early 1990s or will necessarily cause economic problems in the future. It is nevertheless a convenient explanation given that government may desire to cut back spending on seniors.

The aging of the population trend in Alberta implies an increasing seniors' dependency ratio. However, at the same that the seniors' dependency ratio is rising, the youth dependency ratio is falling. In other words, one might wonder why there are not more suggestions for transferring resources from a declining segment of the population – youth – to an increasing segment – seniors. Actually, just the opposite seems to be occurring. That is, concern is being increasingly expressed that seniors already have more than their fair share of resources and that there should be a redistribution in favor of the non-elderly. We continue to live in an agist society, where youth is valued more than age, and where it is frequently argued that seniors should sacrifice for the benefit of young people, but seldom argued that youth should sacrifice for the benefit of the aged. For example, we frequently argue that seniors should accept unemployment (i.e., retirement) so that young people can have jobs and that in return seniors should accept a partial income (i.e., a pension) rather than a whole income. Similarly, there is a tendency to argue that society should cut back programs for seniors so that seniors will not become a burden to non-seniors.

In the twentieth century, seniors were defined into existence by social policies created at a time when political, economic, and social interests were served by the introduction of mechanisms designed to remove seniors from the labor force. Today, political, economic, and social interests are motivated to once again redefine old age. Now that there are economic difficulties, the tendency is to delegitimize old age, to argue that expenditures on seniors must be reduced, and to imply that seniors themselves, given their increasing numbers, are to blame for fiscal problems.

Consider the rising costs of health care. In Alberta, as elsewhere, seniors are disproportionate users of the health care system and the rise in the proportion of seniors is therefore cited as a cause of increasing health care costs. Indeed, the rhetoric often implies that population aging is **the major cause** of rising health care costs. However, once again, this rhetoric scapegoats seniors and creates a rhetorical smokescreen that hides other and more important causes of rising health care costs. The truth is that per capita health care utilization has been increasing for both seniors and non-seniors alike and in recent years, per capita usage has often increased more for non-seniors than for seniors. In other words, there is an upward trend in health care utilization/costs that is separate from the population aging trend. Nevertheless, it is easier and more politically expedient to blame seniors than to look elsewhere (to health care providers, perhaps) for the sources of rising health care costs.

Note that negative stereotyping of seniors in Alberta is simply not supported by the data. For example, only a small minority are heavy users of the health care system. For years, surveys of Alberta's seniors have shown most to be relatively healthy, happy, and able and willing to live independently. Apparently the negative stereotypes about seniors in general are based on the minority who are dying or who suffer from extreme chronic disability, illness, or frailty. Given that the negative stereotypes of older Albertans have been discredited in survey after survey, one wonders why the stereotypes and the associated crisis scenario persist. Apparently, such rhetoric serves to justify the blaming of seniors for fiscal difficulties and serves to justify cuts to programs for seniors.

Ironically, there is a danger that accepting a more positive view of seniors might also be abused. That is, rather than stereotyping all seniors as dependent on public services, redefining seniors in general as **not** in need could also become a justification for cutting funding to seniors, thereby victimizing those needy seniors who do rely on various programs for the aged.

Rising service costs motivate a policy of shifting care from more expensive to less expensive forms, e.g., from institutional care to home care and from professional service providers to voluntary service providers. The accompanying rhetoric stresses the importance and desirability of maintaining seniors' independence and providing a coordinated continuum of care, when care is needed. The "independence" rhetoric is used to justify shifting responsibility for care to the individual and to family members. This shift has the potential for "blaming the victim," who cannot care for him/herself and places inequitable, unrecognized, and unrewarded demands on family caregivers, most of whom are female, given the current gendered division of labor in the family.

The coordination of services rhetoric serves to justify mechanisms that can limit access to care. Note that Alberta has instituted a single point of entry for long term care. Access to long term care is now determined by the local Home Care Program, which administers the Alberta Assessment and Placement Instrument in order to guarantee that seniors will not gain access to expensive care until less expensive care options have been exhausted. While the AAPI is justified as a mechanism that guarantees the independence of seniors for as long as possible, it can also be viewed as a gate-keeping mechanism that could be used to limit access to expensive care. Furthermore, the myth of families refusing to provide care and irresponsibly abandoning their senior members is used to create guilt and to motivate and justify an emphasis on voluntary home care (the cheapest of all alternatives, at least from government's point of view).

The ethic of individual self-reliance and reliance on family is not new. Indeed, this ethic was predominant at the time of the framing of the British North America Act and the birth of Canada as a nation. This ethic served governments well at a time when they did not offer extensive programs for the needy. This ethic is being recreated now that governments find themselves unable to fund the extensive programs that have been designed as part of the modern welfare state. Currently, the Alberta Government increasingly stresses individual self-reliance, reliance on the family, and the maintenance of independence for as long as possible through community-based programs such as Home Care. Even the rhetoric of health care, which emphasizes holistic health, health promotion, and illness prevention, stresses individual responsibility and self-reliance and is touted not only as a better means, but also as a cheaper means, of addressing health issues. Ironically, there is a danger that the holistic health rhetoric will justify an increased, rather than decreased, involvement of health care professionals in our lives. But then, rhetoric is often a two-edged sword.

Income security programs were created and broadened substantially in Canada and in Alberta during the 1927-1985 period. The foreseeable future would seem to be a period of restructuring and retrenchment in these programs. Similarly, an emphasis on the development of a comprehensive and universally accessible health care system has shifted to an emphasis on controlling costs. The Welfare State was created in a time of fiscal advantage. Now fiscal constraints raise questions about the viability of these programs. Given that many of these programs benefit seniors, large provincial and federal budgetary deficits and debt provide considerable incentive and opportunity for the redefinition of old age and the delegitimation of seniors with regards to entitlement to benefits. Furthermore, seniors, who are increasing in number and who are easily stigmatized in an agist society, can be made the scapegoat for fiscal crisis and used to deflect attention away from government, other groups, and from other important issues. In short, the rhetoric of the aging crisis is used to deflect the blame for governmental cuts onto seniors themselves.

The Alberta Government came under considerable pressure in the 1980s and early 1990s, due to a lagging economy and cutbacks in the transfer of federal funds to the province. In its 1994 budget, the Alberta Government announced the restructuring of several programs for seniors into the Alberta Seniors Benefit. This new program effectively ended universal benefits for seniors in Alberta. Only less well-off seniors would qualify for assistance. All other seniors would pay their own way "just like any other Albertan."

Similarly, the federal government has proposed to restructure the Old Age Security and Guaranteed Income Supplement programs in a new Seniors Benefit which will be available only to less well-off seniors. This will end universality at the federal level. Universal age-based programming has been identified as too costly, now and in the future, given population aging trends and a context of fiscal difficulty.

While universal programs for seniors avoid the stigma of income- or means-testing and the appearance of being charity dispensed to the needy, nevertheless, universal age-based programs are coming to a close. In difficult economic times, contributory (merit-) based programs and particularly needs-based programs are more defensible. Universal programs that benefit rich and poor alike appear less defensible. In Alberta, the percentage of seniors receiving the GIS has been declining due to increased coverage from the Canada Pension Plan, private pensions, savings, and so on. In a sense, not only are universal programs under attack, but targeted income security programs such as the GIS are being shifted to contributory programs (such as CPP) and to the private sector (e.g., private pensions and savings).

In summary, in the 1980s Alberta entered a period of fiscal constraint. These economic difficulties have led to a political agenda that involves reducing or limiting governmental expenditures. Indeed, Alberta's 1993 Deficit Elimination Act was followed by massive reductions in government spending over the 1994/95 to 1996/97 period. The population aging trend, socially constructed outside of Alberta as a "crisis," has been adopted in Alberta by government, media, and the public alike. This crisis scenario implies that seniors are a major cause of fiscal difficulty. While population aging in Alberta tends to exacerbate fiscal difficulties, nevertheless, the **primary** causes of the fiscal crisis lie elsewhere. The population aging crisis scenario, however, justifies cuts in expenditures for seniors while at the same time placing blame for these cuts on the growing number of seniors themselves.

The Fiscal Crisis and Intergenerational Equity

In the early 1990s, governments in Canada increasingly acknowledged the problems of continuing deficits and the resulting debt and debt-servicing costs. Indeed, rhetoric emerged increasingly to draw attention to fiscal issues. Some analysts, in turn, began to express concern over the "politics of debt" and a rhetoric that they found excessive or misleading (see, for example, Harrison and Laxer, 1995).

The fiscal crisis rhetoric became so strong in the 1990s that, to an extent, it muted the rhetoric of the population aging crisis, in part by incorporating it. That is, discussions of the fiscal crisis in the mid-1990s tended to include references to the increasing numbers and proportions of seniors in the population, suggesting that population aging will compound fiscal difficulties in the future. In this sense the imagery of a population aging crisis remained. However, the imagery became more implicit than explicit. The prose was "cool," but the imagery that was implied between the lines was "hot." The implied image was that of a grey horde rising in the near future to overwhelm the welfare state and burden a younger generation, who would be required to pay for benefits that it in turn would never receive.

The population aging crisis has been subsumed under the fiscal crisis. The fiscal crisis, in the form of budgetary deficits and resulting debt, has pressured governments to raise tax revenues and to cut program spending. Alberta launched an aggressive strategy in 1993 to eliminate the provincial deficit and to lower the provincial debt. Program spending was reduced dramatically over a three-year period. All areas of government spending, including seniors and health care, endured substantial cuts in program funding. In addition, programs have been fundamentally restructured. Such restructuring requires new rationale and gives rise to new rhetoric.

The federal government has also endorsed a deficit reduction agenda, but has moved much more slowly than provinces like Alberta on this issue. Further, the federal government has not yet come to terms with the massive national debt. Nevertheless, the federal government has succeeded in creating an operating surplus. This means that federal tax revenues exceed program expenditures, ignoring debt-servicing costs. In other words, Canada could afford its existing social programs if the country were not in debt. Indeed, the operating surplus is being used to help pay interest charges on the debt. If it were not for these interest charges, the operating surplus would be available to help pay for the increasing costs of an aging population.

I am arguing that there is a "problem." However, the problem is primarily a fiscal one. Aging, per se, need not be problematic. In a healthy economy, adjustments could be easily made. However, in an unhealthy fiscal context, there is a tendency to focus on population aging as a problem.

The federal debt is so massive that debt-servicing consumes about one out of every three dollars that the federal government spends. When the federal debt is combined with debt at other levels of government, total debt-servicing costs in 1990 exceeded the total cost of the entire health care system in Canada (Northcott, 1993). It would appear that the health care "crisis" and the population aging "crisis" would be non-issues if governments in Canada were not in debt. Seniors are not the central problem. Neither are the sick nor the frail nor the dying particularly problematic. Debt is the central problem, and because of the debt, all else becomes problematic. When large proportions of public revenues must be diverted to pay interest charges on the public debt, then the rising costs of health care or of an aging population do become problematic. Eliminating budgetary deficits and reducing governmental debt will, in time, free up dollars for public spending on social programs. This is the strategy and the rationale employed by the Alberta Government in the mid-1990s. As courses of action are selected, rhetoric creeps in to obscure reality as strategies are justified by some and criticized by others.

Government policy documents in the early 1990s have increasingly emphasized the themes of sustainability and equity. These themes appear to be part of a new and emerging rhetoric. Sustainability refers to the ability to maintain existing programs in the future. The bulk of Canada's social programs are funded on a pay-as-you-go basis. This means that the working generation pays for the benefits of the retired generation. When the working generation retires, its pensions are in turn paid for by the next upcoming generation. It is really a "pyramid scheme." Its success depends on a continuous supply of upcoming generations of sufficient size, wealth, and motivation. The scheme collapses when one runs out of generations, so to speak. That is, if an upcoming generation is relatively small, or unable, or unwilling to "play the game," then all comes crashing down. Pay-as-you-go funding depends on the trust that one generation has in the next generation. A generation will be willing to fund the program as long as it can believe that it will receive benefits in turn from the next generation.

This trust between the generations has been undermined by fiscal difficulties and the rhetoric of the population aging crisis. The common image has been one of apocalypse. That is, the image has been created of a future welfare state bankrupted by seniors who have burdened a younger and over-taxed generation who will soon be disappointed when their own anticipated benefits fail to materialize. The image then is one of intergenerational inequity and age-polarized political strife or "age wars," as the potential conflict has been provocatively labelled.

In other words, references to the issue of sustainability are really references to the issue of intergenerational equity. Until the 1990s, the intergenerational equity theme was more common outside of Canada than it was within Canada (Clark, 1993; Gee and McDaniel, 1993). Indeed, a survey of public opinion in Alberta conducted in the late 1980s found no evidence for intergenerational tension or age-polarization with respect to public policies for supporting an aging population (Northcott, 1994). Nevertheless, governmental documents in Canada and in Alberta in the 1990s increasingly have emphasized the intertwined issues of sustainability and intergenerational equity as justifications for program cutbacks and program restructuring. Sustainability and equity are raised as a future problem. That is, the possibility of future inequity resulting from program unsustainability is cast as a future crisis. This implied impending future crisis is used as a goad and justification for present policy change.

Intergenerational equity has been extensively discussed (see for example, Johnson, 1995; see also the edited collections by Minkler and Estes, 1991 and Myles and Quadagno, 1991). This theme has appeared increasingly in Canada in the 1990s. For example, the 1996 report on the Canada Pension Plan consultations (Federal/Provincial/Territorial CPP Consultations Secretariat, 1996) noted that:

> Many participants in the consultations said that their children and grandchildren would not be in a position to pay such high contribution rates because their legacy is one of poor job prospects and lower incomes. A number argued that it would be unfair to their grandchildren to have to pay 14.2 per cent for exactly the same benefit that the current working generation is paying 5.6 per cent for, and today's seniors paid even less for. (p. 29)

The report then goes on to discuss ways of strengthening the Canada Pension Plan so that it would "fairer across generations" and "more sustainable for future participants" (p. 33).

Good (1995) used a technique called generational accounting to examine issues of sustainability and generational equity in Canada. He concludes that Canada's debt and spending obligations are unsustainable in the long term. Good observes that "The general trend is for older people to receive much more in transfers than they pay in taxes" and that "Future generations must contribute much more to government net revenues than current generations are doing now" (p. 10). Good suggests that a "freeze" on government spending is one possible solution to the problem. It is not my purpose to enter into the debate that such analyses are likely to generate. My point is that analysts and policymakers in Canada in the 1990s are increasingly raising the "spectre" of unsustainability and intergenerational inequity and using this image to justify changes in present public policy.

It does seem clear that fiscal realities coupled with demographic trends do require some adjustments in social programming. What is not clear is the extent to which generational solidarity will be undermined in the future. The "age wars" worst case scenario is but one possibility. More optimistic scenarios are also possible, but of course the worst case scenario best gets people's attention and has considerable motivational potential.

The intergenerational equity theme addresses not only the vested economic interests of separate generations (i.e., the political economy of generational relations) but also addresses the sense of reciprocal obligation that generations tend to feel toward one another. These feelings of obligation and their effect on social policy have been described as a "moral economy" which works in conjunction with the political economy (Minkler and Cole, 1991). The argument is that policy developments tend to reflect not only economic interests and political expediency but also a society's sense of its moral obligations. Perhaps this is why the age wars scenario is so draconian. It envisages not only a political struggle between the generations for scarce economic resources, but also envisions a collapse of the moral order that reciprocally obligates and solidifies the generations.

The collapse of social solidarity is a recurring, though largely implicit, thesis. While intergenerational equity focuses on solidarity between generations, solidarity between social classes and between the genders has also been called into question. As age-based universal programming for seniors (such as the OAS in Canada, or health care premium and property tax waivers in Alberta) is eliminated and replaced with targeted programs for less well-off seniors only, questions about cross-class solidarity are raised. As health care for seniors is shifted from institutions to community and from professionals to family, questions about gender equity are raised.

Quadagno (1991) discusses the middle-class incorporation thesis. She suggests that a social assistance model for social welfare primarily taxes the middle class but primarily benefits the working class. This model provides little incentive for the middle class to support such programs. On the other hand, Quadagno suggests that a social security model that provides universal benefits tends to unite working class and middle class interests and create cross-class solidarity. Universal programs also remove the stigma of means- or income-testing to determine who needs assistance. With universality, the poor are not identified as such and are not subjected to the indignity of being offered "charity." Universal benefits tend to be defined as a "right" to which all are entitled.

In Canada and in Alberta, age-based universal programs are being eliminated and replaced with targeted programs for needy seniors only. In Quadnago's terms, the social security model is being replaced with a social assistance model. While this shift in policy reduces the number of beneficiaries and the costs of supporting seniors, at the same time this policy change divides the interests of the middle and working classes. Middle class support for programs that benefit only the working class will tend to be eroded. Cross-class solidarity may be undermined and politics may become increasingly class-polarized. In addition, targeting may reduce the incentive to provide for oneself while at the same time increasing the resentment of those who do.

Just as targeting may increase tension between the classes, so also might the shift from institutional care to family care models create tension between men and women. The gender division of labor has assigned the work of caregiving primarily to women. Women are expected to forego careers, income, benefits, and pensions in order to provide care in the home. This care is unrewarded, unremunerated, and too often unrecognized. As women struggle to overcome gender inequity, the healthcare and eldercare policies of the 1990s will seem retrogressive. Indeed, unless the burden of caring for seniors in the home and community is shared more equally by men and women, one might expect an increased tension between the genders.

In summary, the emerging themes of (un)sustainability and intergenerational (in)equity tend to paint a dismal picture for the future. The sustainability theme argues that fiscal difficulties coupled with population aging mean that current social programs are not sustainable in the long term. Fundamental change is required if social programs are to be viable in the future. If these changes are not made, social solidarity will collapse as one generation struggles with another, as social classes polarize, and as resentment between the genders builds. Ironically, the strategies being implemented in the 1990s may also undermine social solidarity. The elimination of universal age-based programs, targeting benefits to the most needy, and shifting caregiving to the home and family may precipitate class- and gender-polarization. In such a political climate, younger generations may wonder if programs will survive to assist them in their time of need. And of course, younger middle class persons might have little commitment to programs that they do not expect to ever need or benefit from.

Myth and the Social Construction of Reality in Alberta

Others have explored the rhetoric-versus-reality theme. Jefferys (1983), writing about the over-eighty year olds in Britain, discusses the "social construction of panic." She notes that a projected 50% increase in the number of 80+ year olds from 1980 to 2001 has created "something of a panic" as if there is a "disaster" looming (p. 368). Jefferys singles out the media for painting "gloomy pictures" of a forthcoming and overwhelming "extra burden." Nevertheless, Jefferys points out that the projected increase in 80+ year olds amounts to only an additional 4 persons per 1000!! Surely, Jefferys argues, this is not cause for such alarm; indeed, Jefferys wonders why there appears to be so little concern about "large-scale structural unemployment," for example, which would seem to be a far greater problem (p. 369).

Minkler (1983) argues that the fiscal conservatism of the United States in the 1980s has led to the "blaming of the aged victim." That is, she suggests that American seniors are being blamed for fiscal crisis in the United States. Further, it is not only the growing number of seniors which is perceived as problematic but also the very programs designed to assist seniors which are perceived as bankrupting the country. Minkler argues that seniors are being scapegoated and used as a smokescreen to direct attention from other issues such as unemployment, a sluggish economy, military expenditures, and the self-interest of corporate business. In short, Minkler suggests that the definition of old age is socially constructed, arising from the interplay of various economic, political, and social forces. The current definition of old age, according to Minkler, tends to victimize seniors as a result of "the politics of scapegoating."

McDaniel (1987) argues that population aging has emerged in the 1980s as a prominent "problem paradigm" (a paradigm is a model of social reality). She suggests that a number of issues in areas as diverse as health care, the economy, and immigration policy, for example, have come to be associated with the "problem" of population aging. McDaniel notes that the "process of paradigm-making" is a result of the interplay (a "circuitous process of mutual reinforcement") between social scientists, policymakers, and the media (p. 331). She describes a bandwagon effect, wherein a social consensus develops that an issue "must be important because so many people are talking about it." In other words, a problem paradigm can "take on a reality of [its] own after a time, whether or not [it] had any solid basis in reality initially" (p. 331). McDaniel goes on to argue that population aging is such a paradigm. She notes that population aging has come to be viewed as a central social problem explaining many other social and economic problems. She points out that this simplistic model confuses causes and consequences, overly simplifies complex linkages, and allows many of the actual causes of various social problems to be overlooked.

Similarly, Evans (1987b; see also 1987a) describes the "rhetoric of a 'crisis' of aging" as a veil which obscures the various causes of rising health care costs and fosters "illusions of necessity," which tend to serve vested interests in the health care delivery system. In other words, Evans argues that there is a tendency to assume that population aging is a major and inevitable determinant of rising health care costs. This assumption deflects attention away from the various ways in which the healthcare delivery system itself influences costs. Barer, et al. (1986 and 1987) make similar arguments in articles subtitled "Rhetoric and Evidence" and "New Evidence on Old Fallacies." Finally, Evans (1989:146) notes that policy questions such as population aging have a way of becoming burdensome policy problems that become obscured by "a considerable amount of rhetorical fog."

Freer (1988) discusses various myths and misconceptions about seniors. He notes the prevalence of "worse case examples," negative stereotypes, and agism and complains that in the professional and lay press: "The titles, headlines, and contents of most articles still reflect an atmosphere of crisis, exploding numbers and impending overwhelming demand whenever the subject of the growing number of older people in contemporary society is discussed" (p. 3). Freer goes on to discuss common myths regarding the health of seniors, the risks of living alone, the extent and availability of family support, and so on.

The dynamics of population aging in Alberta and elsewhere are well understood, although popular myths persist. For example, the cause of population aging is often thought to be increasing life expectancy associated with rising standards of living and better health. This argument tends to be expressed simply as follows: A greater proportion of the population is elderly because people are living longer. This statement misleads in two respects. First of all, the statement "people are living longer" is ambiguous. Does this statement imply that everyone, even seniors, are living significantly longer today? Or does this statement imply that a greater proportion of people are surviving to reach old age? The first interpretation implies changes in the human life span (the average number of years a person can expect to live under ideal circumstances) while the second interpretation refers to changes in life expectancy (the average number of years a person can expect to live under actual circumstances). While life expectancy has indeed increased, it is not at all clear that the life span has changed much, if at all.

The difference between life span and life expectancy notwithstanding, the statement "people are living longer" implies that declining mortality is the essential cause of population aging. This brings us to the second error. Even if every person lived out his/her full and natural life span, as long as there was a high rate of birth, old people would remain a relatively small percentage of the total population. In other words, increasing life expectancy (coupled with high fertility) gives rise not to population aging but rather to the so-called "population explosion." Historically, the aging of the population has tended to come later, as birth rates decline. In short, while it is true that people on average are living longer (i.e., life expectancy has increased, meaning that a greater percentage are surviving into old age), nevertheless, the cause of population aging first and foremost is declining rates of fertility. The truth is that the population is aging not so much because people are living longer but rather because people are having fewer children.

The Future of Population Aging in Alberta

There is no doubt that the population of Canada and the population of Alberta are aging. Furthermore, it is expected that this aging trend will continue well into the twenty-first century. While the previous discussion has examined the current definition of and response to population aging, the following question remains: what are the future implications of the aging trend? As argued previously, the rhetoric applied to this question tends to use terms such as "problem," "challenge," or "crisis." Certainly, the aging of the population will place various pressures on service delivery systems and might seem to require a redistribution of economic and social resources. Whether such pressures constitute a "problem" or a "challenge," and whether such pressures will lead to a "crisis" of some sort or not depends heavily on one's point of view.

Just the same, there has been a tendency to think of population aging as problematic for the future. For example, there is a tendency to assume that population aging will lead to various future problems such as a shortage of long term care beds or rising taxes. Again, this argument misleads. While it is true that population aging does have implications for future service delivery and costs, as well as for tax revenues and so on, population aging is not the only factor and may not even be the most important factor influencing future service delivery issues (Evans, 1987a, 1987b, 1989). Population aging has become something of a bogeyman, singled out as the problem while other relevant factors are mini- mized or overlooked (McDaniel, 1987; Evans, 1987a, 1987b, 1989). Other factors such as technological change, proliferation of the types and numbers of professional caregivers, the vested interests of professionals and institutions, provider-initiated servicing patterns, changing consumer demands, labor force trends, economic trends, and so on will all play a role in determining whether or not there is a future crisis.

Much of the debate concerning the future service delivery implications of population aging is based on assumptions about the needs of the elderly population. For example, seniors are disproportionate users of health care services. This statistical fact fuels misperceptions. While seniors may be at greater risk for health care and other problems, study after study has shown that the great majority of seniors are healthy, happy, and able to live independently. Even at an advanced age, most seniors are able to live independently or with a modest amount of assistance from informal or formal sources. Furthermore, the great bulk of assistance is supplied informally (mostly by family members) rather than by the formal delivery system. In other words, if there is a problem, it is not with all seniors, but rather with the relatively small percentage of seniors who have become dependent for reasons such as declining health, inadequate financial resources, or lack of informal social supports.

Ironically, despite the stereotypes that tend to portray seniors collectively as sick, poor, isolated, and dependent, there is a recent rhetoric that is just as optimistic for the future as the old stereotypes are pessimistic. Consider the current rhetoric that emphasizes the "prevention" of problems and the "promotion" of health. This rhetoric promises that prevention and promotion strategies can result in significant improvements in the health of seniors. In other words, there is an expectation that old people will be healthier in the future, or at least healthier longer. Again, the rhetoric misleads. To date, this argument (more formally known as the compression or rectangularization of morbidity hypothesis) has failed to receive unequivocal empirical support. It remains a highly optimistic notion that appeals to those who dream of better tomorrows and that justifies those who are caught up in the current prevention and promotion ideology.

If population aging is defined as problematic in some way, then it follows that one might consider various solutions to the problem. If the cause of the problem is declining or low fertility, then perhaps the solution is to raise fertility. However, governmental attempts to influence fertility are not likely to be effective (McDaniel, 1987:334). Alternatively, the problem might be perceived to be the ratio of the dependent population to the independent (i.e., taxpaying) population. If this is the case, then perhaps the solution is to increase the labor force by means of increased immigration and/or encouraging seniors to remain in the labor force longer. However, increasing immigration is not likely to be popular and retirement patterns are rather firmly entrenched, with a preference for earlier rather than later retirement.

If the problem is perceived to be increasing demand for services as a consequence of an increasing proportion of seniors, then it is often suggested that the solution is to lower demand for services through prevention and health promotion strategies. However, as noted above, the image of a long, healthy, and happy life ending naturally, peacefully, quickly, and inexpensively at a ripe old age remains a utopian dream for most. If the problem is perceived to be increasing costs associated with an aging population, then it is argued that the solution is to substitute less expensive (but allegedly better!!) services, e.g., community-based care instead of facility-based care. In short, different perceptions of what is problematic about population aging suggest different solutions.

I have suggested that the problematic nature of population aging has been inadequately defined. For example, as noted earlier, only a small percentage of the aged account for the high proportion of resources spent on seniors. Perhaps the problem, if there is a problem, relates not to resources invested in seniors generally, but rather relates to the resources spent on relatively small groups of seniors, on the dying, for example. Perhaps the important issues are questions such as: Are the resources spent on the dying justified? How could these costs be reduced? How does one decide who will receive what treatment? and so on.

Perhaps there is **not** a population aging problem. After all, Alberta has a relatively low percentage of seniors compared to the other provinces in Canada and compared to "older" nations such as many of the European countries. Given that these "older" jurisdictions seem to have coped quite well with their aging populations, it seems likely that Alberta will also manage reasonably well. Furthermore, an aging population might well have its advantages. For example, seniors represent a relatively large pool of discretionary income and investment capital. Seniors also constitute a substantial potential volunteer labor force, with the time, skills, and often the inclination to participate in various aspects of community life. In short, a large aged population may well turn out to be both an economic and a social asset.

There is other rhetoric that can be challenged. For example, one might hear it said that population aging is primarily and/or increasingly a female problem. While it is true that female life expectancy currently exceeds male life expectancy and as a consequence there are generally more older women than older men, and while it is true that older women are more likely than older men to be widowed, poor, dependent, and institutionalized, nevertheless these generalizations cannot be applied universally. For example, these statements do not apply equally to all parts of Alberta. Consider parts of northern Alberta, where older men outnumber older women. Further, there are indications that the life expectancy of males may be beginning to catch up, to a degree at least, with female life expectancy. Should this trend continue, sex ratios will converge in time to some degree. In addition, the increasing involvement of women in the labor force implies that older women in the future will be less dependent economically than older women today. In other words, these trends imply that aging may become somewhat more equitable for the sexes in the future, rather than less equitable. It is and will be a mistake to identify the problems of aging solely with one sex or the other. It is, of course, also wrong to ignore gender differentials where and when they exist.

It is becoming clear that the notion that the modern family lacks the will and/or resources to care for senior family members is also erroneous. Most seniors report that their families either already do or are willing to provide needed assistance. Indeed, it is known that the great bulk of assistance that is provided to seniors comes from informal (mostly family) sources rather than from the formal service delivery system. An equally misleading corollary to the notion that the modern family cannot or will not care for its dependent aged is the allegation that the modern family "forces" its dependent seniors into facilities.

There is evidence that most seniors **prefer** lodge accommodation or nursing home placement to moving in with their adult children. An exception to this generalization appears to be Native elders, who prefer to live with their extended families rather than be separated from their kin and from their communities through placement in long-term care facilities.

Whatever the reality, generally it is the perception that there must be changes in the way we deliver services to seniors. The combination of population aging, increases in service delivery costs, governmental budget deficits, and high debt servicing costs raises concerns about our ability to support seniors in the future. The contemporary rhetoric contains a number of catch-phrases that describe the reforms that are being proposed and implemented to deal with the aging of the population. The "evils" of unnecessary or excessive dependency and/or premature placement in a long-term care facility tend to be raised as a justification for proposed reforms. Further, it is argued that the service emphasis must be shifted to encourage independence, self-reliance, individual responsibility, and informal social supports. In an effort to promote these goals, it is argued that the emphasis be shifted from facility-based care to community-based care and that a full continuum of care be offered with a single point of entry to facilitate coordination and appropriate referral/placement. In other words, there is a joint emphasis on individual self-reliance on the one hand and on collective responsibility for caring for the needy on the other hand. Nevertheless, the primary emphasis is to be on self-reliance and on minimizing the level of care offered/utilized.

These reforms have two central motivations. It is hoped that these changes will improve the quality of life of seniors generally and it is also hoped that these changes will result in a reduction in service delivery costs (where "reduction" might mean either lower total costs, lower costs to government, lower per capita costs, or a slowing in the rate of increase in costs). Both of these motivations – the humanitarian and the economic – are closely intertwined, although there is a tendency for the rhetoric to emphasize the humanitarian arguments over the economic.

One could ask whether the economic concerns led to cost-cutting proposals which have been "sold" as humanitarian reforms, or whether humanitarian concerns led to proposed reforms which have the added "selling feature" of appearing to promise cost reductions. Whatever the answer, it is important to note that current rhetoric promises both better services and reduced costs. Perhaps both goals can be achieved, although generally, one should be wary of schemes that promise more for less. Perhaps the argument that both can be accomplished simultaneously is wishful thinking on the part of the sincere or a cynical sell on the part of the insincere. Certainly costs could be reduced if services are rationed aggressively in the name of independence and self-reliance. But would this result in a better state of affairs for seniors?

Alternatively, consider the ideals of prevention, health promotion, complete mental/physical/social well-being, and health for all. While such contemporary rhetoric promises a better future, nevertheless, can such open-ended goals result in cost-savings? Do they not rather invite the proliferation of professionals seeking an increased mandate to influence our individual lives and demanding increasingly large commitments from the public purse?

Many questions remain to be answered. There is an existing service delivery system with powerful and entrenched vested interests. Can the momentum of this system be overcome and the caregiving emphasis shifted? The proposed shift in emphasis promises cost savings and better care. Can both be attained or can cost savings be attained only at the expense of quality of care? The proposed emphasis on health promotion promises fewer health care needs and therefore reduced costs. Can such a utopian promise be accomplished and at a reduction in overall costs? In regards to income security programs, will the elimination of universal age-based benefits and the emphasis on programs targeted only to the "needy" continue to receive support from rich and poor, young and old, and male and female? The answers to these questions remain shrouded in an uncertain future. Nevertheless, the eventual answers to these questions will depend more on trends in the economy and in the service delivery system than on the population aging trend itself.

Notes

Notes to Chapter 2

1. The "living will" is more formally known as an "advance directive." The Alberta Government has proposed new legislation called the Advance Directives Act which would make living wills legally binding (see Alberta Health, 1994a for a discussion paper on this proposal). As of August, 1996, this Act had not been passed by the Alberta Legislature.

2. Section 15, subsection 1 of the Canadian Charter of Rights and Freedoms forbids discrimination on the basis of age; however, subsection 2 allows affirmative action programs for the economically or socially disadvantaged (McBlane, 1982). Nevertheless, the question is: "Are all seniors disadvantaged?" If the answer is "No", then universal programs for the aged may be deemed discriminatory in that they provide all seniors with services and advantages not offered to non-seniors. Means-tested or income-tested programs would survive, presumably, but universal programs might well come under attack. While universal programs for seniors have come under attack in the 1990s, the reasons given usually focus on the financial costs rather than on the legal aspects of such programs and the need for targeting scarce dollars to needy seniors.

   In Alberta, the Individual's Rights Protection Act, originally passed in 1972, prohibits age discrimination in employment for persons 18 years of age and older. Nevertheless, mandatory retirement has been found to be acceptable, for example, for work groups such as firefighters and professors.

3. Alternatives for subdividing Alberta geographically include the 19 census divisions (CDs), the various census subdivisions (cities, towns, villages, counties), and, since 1994, the 17 regional health authorities.

4. Tables 2-5 and 2-6 report 1991 census data. At the time of writing, detailed information from the 1996 census was not yet available.

5. The 1994 edition of *Older Albertans* was cancelled due to government cutbacks. The 1996 edition is expected in 1997 following the release of 1996 census data.

6. This emphasis on wealth could be recast as a discussion of "needs." That is, if a person owns a house "free and clear," then that person does not "need" the income that another person would require to make mortgage payments. Further, seniors often have already made their major furniture and appliance purchases and have finished raising their children (although some have noted that you never finish raising your children). The point is, seniors may require less income to maintain a given lifestyle than someone just starting out in adult life.

Notes to Chapter 3

1. Calculated from data in Table 17, *Alberta Health: Statistical Supplement 1994-95*, (Edmonton: Alberta Health Care Insurance Plan, Alberta Health, 1995).

2. The Health Promotion Survey conducted by Health and Welfare Canada was to be scheduled every five years. The second cycle was conducted in 1990. A total of 2600

Albertans 15 years of age and older was surveyed. The sample for the Southern Region of the province was augmented.

3. The General Social Survey is an annual survey of approximately 10 000 persons aged 15 and over, excluding residents of institutions. The first survey (1985), which can be compared to the 1978/79 Canada Health Survey, focused on the health status of the population and also on social support for seniors. The elderly population was oversampled (n = 3150 persons 65+ years of age). The second survey (1986) focused on time use while the third survey (1988) examined accidents and victimization. The fourth survey (1989) studied education and work. The fifth survey (1990), like the first, involved an oversampling of seniors. The 1990 survey examined family issues including contacts with family and friends and giving and receiving assistance. The General Social Survey rotates through these five topics on a 5-year repeating cycle.

Notes to Chapter 4

1. From October 1994 through May 1996, the Council was assigned to Alberta Health, returning to Community Development in June of 1996.

Notes to Chapter 5

1. The year in which legislation is passed and the year in which it is implemented are often different. The Old Age Security Act and the Old Age Assistance Act were passed in 1951 and implemented in 1952.

2. Myles (1988:41) gives the year as 1967. As noted in footnote 1 above, the year in which legislation is passed and the year in which it is implemented are often different.

3. Myles (1988:40) gives the year as 1965.

4. In July of 1996, the federal government, which had been mailing OAS cheques to wealthier seniors, only to "claw" them back fully or partially at tax time, simply began deducting the clawback from the cheques (National Council of Welfare, 1996c:4). This meant that, for the wealthiest seniors, the OAS cheque was no longer sent at all.

References

Aboriginal Health Unit, Alberta Health
    n.d.   *Strengthening the Circle: What Aboriginal Albertans Say About Their Health*. Edmonton.

Alberta Bureau of Statistics
    1988   *Population Projections, Alberta, 1987-2016*. Edmonton.

Alberta Community and Occupational Health
    n.d.   *Moving into the Future: For the Health of Albertans*. Edmonton.

Alberta Council on Aging
    1983   *Project Involvement: Community Work With Seniors in Alberta*. Edmonton.

Alberta Health
    1995a   *Population Projections by Health Region 1991 to 1996*. Edmonton.
    1995b   *Healthy Albertans Living in a Healthy Alberta: A Three-Year Business Plan 1995-96 to 1997-98*. Edmonton.
    1994a   *Decisions about Tomorrow: Directives for Your Health Care. Discussion Paper*. Edmonton.
    1994b   *Healthy Albertans Living in a Healthy Alberta: A Three-Year Business Plan*. Edmonton.
    1992   *Home Care in Alberta: New Directions in Community Support*. Edmonton.
    1991   *Report of the Alberta Heart Health Survey*. Edmonton.

Alberta Health Facilities Review Committee
    1991   *Foundations for the Future: The 1990 Senior Citizens' Lodge Survey*. Edmonton.

Alberta Health, Health Economics, and Statistics
    1991   *Dimensions of Disability in Alberta: Results of the Health and Activity Limitation Survey (HALS) 1986*. Edmonton.

Alberta Health Planning Secretariat
    1993   *Starting Points: Recommendations for Creating a More Accountable and Affordable Health System*. Edmonton.

Alberta Housing and Public Works
    1977   *Senior Citizens Housing Needs Study: An Analysis of Calgary Waiting Lists*. Edmonton.

Alberta Human Resources Development Authority
    1971   *Senior Citizen Study: Lesser Slave Lake "Special Area"*.

Alberta Indian Health Care Commission
    n.d.   *Survey of Indian Elders on Reserve, August, 1989*.

Alberta Law Reform Institute
    1993   *Advance Directives and Substitute Decision-Making in Personal Healthcare. A Joint Report of The Alberta Law Reform Institute and The Health Law Institute*. Report No. 64. Edmonton.

Alberta Ministry Responsible for Seniors
  1992   *Looking to the Future: A Discussion Paper on an Agenda for Older Albertans.* 2 Volumes. Edmonton.

Alberta Municipal Affairs
  1987   *Summary Findings: Senior Citizen Lodge Program Review.* Edmonton.

Alberta Senior Citizens Secretariat
  1989a   *Alberta's Aging Population: Trends and Implications.* Edmonton.
  1989b   *Older Albertans, 1988.* Edmonton.
  1985   Living Wills: A Background Paper. Edmonton.

Alberta Treasury
  1995   *Public Accounts 1994-95.* Edmonton.
  1994   *Public Accounts 1993-94.* Edmonton.

Angus Reid Associates
  1986   *Qualitative Research on the Health Information Needs of Elderly Albertans.* Edmonton: Alberta Alcohol and Drug Abuse Commission.

Antonovsky, Aaron
  1980   *Health, Stress, and Coping.* San Francisco: JosseyBass.

Associated Planning Consultants Inc.
  1983   *Needs of the Elderly: Medicine Hat.* Vols. 1 and 2. Toronto.

Author Unknown
  1986   *Health and Educational Survey of Seniors in Hanna, Alberta.*

Barer, Morris L., Robert G. Evans, and Clyde Hertzman
  1995   "Avalanche or Glacier? Health Care and the Demographic Rhetoric." *Canadian Journal on Aging,* 14:193-224.

Barer, Morris L., Robert G. Evans, Clyde Hertzman, and Jonathan Lomas
  1987   "Aging and Health Care Utilization: New Evidence on Old Fallacies." *Social Science and Medicine,* 24:851-862.
  1986   "Toward Efficient Aging: Rhetoric and Evidence." Unpublished paper prepared for the Third Canadian Conference on Health Economics, Winnipeg, May 29-30, 1986.

Bassi, Gurmail Singh
  1995   *Public Housing and Nursing Care: A Needs Assessment Survey of South-Asians in Edmonton, 1994-95. Final Report.* Edmonton: The Millwoods Cultural Society of the Retired and Semi-Retired.

Beaujot, Roderic
  1991   *Population Change in Canada: The Challenges of Policy Adaptation.* Toronto: McClelland and Stewart.

Berger, Peter L., and Thomas Luckmann
  1966   *The Social Construction of Reality.* Garden City, N.Y.: Doubleday.

Bergob, Michael
  1994   "Drug Use Among Senior Canadians." *Canadian Social Trends,* Summer:25-29.

Birch, Norman E., and Susan H. Koroluk
  1974   *Study of the Continuum of Care for Senior Adults in Alberta: A Survey and Analysis of Extant Alberta Readings, and a Survey of Senior Citizens.* Edmonton.

Black, Charlyn
  1995   "Using Existing Data Sets to Study Aging and the Elderly: An Introduction." *Canadian Journal on Aging,* 14: 135-150.

Black, Charlyn, Noralou P. Roos, Betty Havens, and Leonard MacWilliam
    1995   "Rising Use of Physician Services by the Elderly: The Contribution of
            Morbidity." *Canadian Journal on Aging*, 14:225-244.

Blair, Deborah I.M.
    1981   *Use of Formal and Informal Support Resources by the Elderly in a
            Rural Community.* M.Sc. Thesis. Calgary: University of Calgary.

Bland, R.C., S.C. Newman, and H. Orn
    1988   "Prevalence of Psychiatric Disorders in the Elderly in Edmonton." *Acta
            Psychiatrica Scandinavica*, 77 (supplement 338): 57-63.

Boyack, Virginia J., Lynda M. McKenzie, and Ellen K. Hansell
    1995   *Synergy II: A Demonstration Project to Address the Issues of Violence
            in Older Families.* Calgary: Kerby Centre.

Brown, Robert L.
    1991   *Economic Security in an Aging Population.* Toronto: Butterworths.

Burke, Mary Anne
    1991   "Implications of an Aging Society." *Canadian Social Trends*, Spring:6-8.

Bury, Mike
    1988   "Arguments About Aging: Long Life and its Consequences." In
            Nicholas Wells and Charles Freer, (eds.), *The Aging Population:
            Burden or Challenge?* London: MacMillan.

Calgary Health Services
    1995   *Health of Calgarians 1995.* Calgary.

Calgary Social Services Department
    1983   *A Profile of the Elderly in Calgary: A Demographic Profile and Needs
            Assessment.* Calgary.

Canada Fitness Survey
    1982   *Fitness and Aging.* Ottawa: Fitness Canada.

Canada Health Survey, Health and Welfare Canada, and Statistics Canada
    1981   *The Health of Canadians: Report of Canada Health Survey.* Ottawa:
            Minister of Supply and Services.

Canadian Study of Health and Aging
    1994   "Patterns of Caring for People with Dementia in Canada," *Canadian
            Journal on Aging*, 13:470-487.

Canadian Study of Health and Aging Working Group
    1994   "Canadian Study of Health and Aging: Study Methods and Prevalence
            of Dementia." *Canadian Medical Association Journal*, 150:899-913.

Chappell, Neena L.
    1987   "Canadian Income and HealthCare Policy: Implications for the Elderly."
            In V.W. Marshall, (ed.), *Aging in Canada: Social Perspectives.* 2nd
            edition. Markham, Ontario: Fitzhenry and Whiteside.

Chappell, Neena L., Laurel A. Strain, and Audrey A. Blandford
    1986   *Aging and Health Care: A Social Perspective.* Toronto: Holt, Rinehart
            and Winston.

Charles, Cathy, and Corinne Schalm
    1992a   "Alberta's Resident Classification System for Long-Term Care
            Facilities. Part I: Conceptual and Methodological Development,"
            Canadian Journal on Aging, 11:219-232.
    1992b   "Alberta's Resident Classification System for Long-Term Care

Facilities. Part II: First-Year Results and Policy Implications,"
Canadian Journal on Aging, 11:233-248.

City of Fort McMurray
    1988   *Fort McMurray Senior Citizens Needs Assessment Survey*. Fort
            McMurray.

Clark, Phillip G.
    1993   "Moral Discourse and Public Policy in Aging: Framing Problems,
            Seeking Solutions, and 'Public Ethics'." *Canadian Journal on Aging*,
            12:485-508.

Committee on Long Term Care for Senior Citizens (Dianne Mirosh, Chairman)
    1988   *A New Vision for Long Term Care – Meeting the Need*. Edmonton:
            Government of Alberta.

Connidis, Ingrid A.
    1989   *Family Ties and Aging*. Toronto: Butterworths.
    1987   "Life in Older Age: The View from the Top." In V.W. Marshall, (ed.),
            Aging in Canada: Social Perspectives, 2nd edition. Markham, Ontario:
            Fitzhenry and Whiteside.
    1983   "Living Arrangement Choices of Older Residents: Assessing
            Quantitative Results with Qualitative Data." *Canadian Journal of
            Sociology*, 8:359-375.

Cuyler, Anthony J.
    1988   *Health Care Expenditures in Canada: Myth and Reality; Past and
            Future*. Canadian Tax paper No. 82. Toronto: Canadian Tax
            Foundation.

deCocq, Gustave A., and Stephanie C. Macleod
    1980   *The Role and Function of Senior Citizen's Lodges in the Metropolitan
            Calgary Foundation*. Calgary: Metropolitan Calgary Foundation.

Denton, Frank T., Christine H. Feaver, and Byron G. Spencer
    1987   "The Canadian Population and Labor Force: Retrospect and Prospect."
            In V.W. Marshall, (ed.), *Aging in Canada: Social Perspectives*. 2nd
            edition. Markham, Ontario: Fitzhenry and Whiteside.
    1986   "Prospective Aging of the Population and Its Implications for the Labor
            Force and Government Expenditures." *Canadian Journal on Aging*,
            5:75-98.

Denton, Frank T., S. Neno Li, and Byron G. Spencer
    1987   "How Will Population Aging Affect the Future Costs of Maintaining
            HealthCare Standards?" In V.W. Marshall, (ed.), *Aging in Canada.
            Social Perspectives*. 2nd edition. Markham, Ontario: Fitzhenry and
            Whiteside.

Denton, Frank T., and Byron G. Spencer
    1995   "Demographic Change and the Cost of Publicly Funded Health Care."
            Canadian Journal on Aging, 14:174-192.
    1980a   "Canada's Population and Labor Force: Past, Present, and Future." In
            V.W. Marshall, (ed.), *Aging in Canada: Social Perspectives*. Don Mills,
            Ontario: Fitzhenry and Whiteside.
    1980b   "Healthcare Costs when the Population Changes." In V.W. Marshall,
            (ed.), *Aging in Canada: Social Perspectives*. Don Mills, Ontario:
            Fitzhenry and Whiteside.

Department of Finance Canada
1996   *Budget 1996: Budget in Brief.* Ottawa.
1991   *The Deficit and the Public Debt.* Ottawa.

Department of National Health and Welfare and Dominion Bureau of Statistics
1960   *Illness and Health Care in Canada, Canadian Sickness Survey 1950-51.*
Ottawa: Queen's Printer.

Devereaux, Mary Sue
1993   "Time Use of Canadians in 1992." *Canadian Social Trends,*
Autumn:13-16.

Dholakia, Jagruti, Mathew Zacharia, and John McNeill
1987   *Problems of South Asian Seniors Living in Calgary.* University of
Calgary: Faculty of Education.

Dinning, Jim
1994   *Budget '94: Securing Alberta's Future.* Edmonton: Government of
Alberta.

Dunn, Peter A.
1991   "Seniors with Disabilities." *Canadian Social Trends,* Spring:14-16.
1990   *Barriers Confronting Seniors with Disabilities in Canada: Special
Topic Series from the Health and Activity Limitation Survey.* Catalogue
No. 82-615. Volume I. Ottawa; Minister of Industry, Science, and
Technology.

Edmonton *Journal*
1996   "It's budget time again," Sunday, March 3:F1.
1996   "Want a tax break?" Friday, February 23:A1.
1996   "Surprise surpluses quicken pace of climb out of debt," Friday,
February 23:A4.
1996   "How much is the debt, anyway?" Thursday, June 27:A8.

Edmonton Social Services, Mill Creek Centre
1989   *Seniors Community Project,* Edmonton.

Edmonton Social Services, Westmount Centre
n.d.   *Senior's Need Survey: Westmount Centre.* Edmonton.

Ehrlich, Paul
1968   *The Population Bomb.* New York: Ballantine.

Elliot, Gail, with the assistance of Melanie Hunt and Kim Hutchison
1996   *Facts on Aging in Canada.* Hamilton: Office of Gerontological Studies,
McMaster University.

Engelmann, Fred C.
1995   "Seniors: The End of a Dream." In Trevor Harrison and Gordon Laxer,
(eds.), *The Trojan Horse: Alberta and the Future of Canada.* Montreal:
Black Rose Books. Pages 286-300.

Engelmann, Mary
1987   *Alberta's Older Population: Present and Future.* Edmonton.

Epp, Jake
1986   *Achieving Health For All: A Framework for Health Promotion.* Ottawa:
Minister of Supply and Services Canada.

Estes, Carroll L.
1991   "The Reagan Legacy: Privatization, the Welfare State, and Aging in the
1990s." In John Myles and Jill Quadagno, (eds.), *State, Labor Markets,
and the Future of Old-Age Policy.* Philadelphia: Temple University

Press.

1984   "Austerity and Aging: 1980 and Beyond." In M. Minkler and C.L.
        Estes, (eds.), *Readings in the Political Economy of Aging*. Farmingdale,
        New York: Baywood.

1983   "Social Security: The Social Construction of a Crisis." *Milbank
        Memorial Fund Quarterly*, 61:445-461.

1979   *The Aging Enterprise*. San Francisco: Jossey-Bass.

Estes, Carroll L., James H. Swan, and Lenore E. Gerard.

1982   "Dominant and Competing Paradigms in Gerontology: Towards a
        Political Economy of Aging." *Ageing and Society*, 2(1982): 151-164.

Estes, Carroll L., Lenore E. Gerard, Jane Sprague Zones, and James H. Swan

1984   *Political Economy, Health, and Aging*. Boston: Little, Brown.

Evans, Robert G.

1989   "Reading the Menu with Better Glasses: Aging and Health Policy
        Research." In S.J. Lewis, (ed.), *Aging and Health: Linking Research
        and Public Policy*. Chelsea, Michigan: Lewis.

1987a   "Hang Together or Hang Separately: The Viability of a Universal
        Health Care System in an Aging Society." *Canadian Public Policy*,
        13:165-180.

1987b   "Illusions of Necessity: Evading Responsibility for Choice in Health
        Care." In D. Coburn, et al. (eds.), *Health and Canadian Society:
        Sociological Perspectives*, 2nd edition. Markham, Ontario: Fitzhenry
        and Whiteside.

Federal/Provincial/Territorial CPP Consultations Secretariat

1996   *Report on the Canada Pension Plan Consultations*. Ottawa: Department
        of Finance.

Feldman, Jacob J.

1983   "Work Ability of the Aged Under Conditions of Improving Mortality."
        Milbank Memorial Fund Quarterly, 61:430-44.

Foot, David K.

1982   *Canada's Population Outlook: Demographic Futures and Economic
        Challenges*. Toronto: Lorimer.

Forbes, Dorothy

1994   *Review of Light Care Residents in Long Term Care Facilities and
        Individuals on the Long Term Care Facility Wait List in the Vegreville
        Region*. Vegreville: Vegreville Long Term Care Centre.

Freer, Charles

1988   "Old Myths: Frequent Misconceptions about the Elderly." In N. Wells
        and C. Freer, (eds.), *The Ageing Population: Burden or Challenge?*
        London: MacMillan.

Fries, James F.

1983   "The Compression of Morbidity." *Milbank Memorial Fund Quarterly*,
        61:397-419.

1980   "Aging, Natural Death, and the Compression of Morbidity." *New
        England Journal of Medicine*, 303 (July 17):130-135.

Frog Lake Band Family and Community Support Services

1983   *Senior Citizens Outreach Program*.

Fuez, Karen

1972   *Characteristics and Lifestyle of People Aged Sixty-Five Years and Over
        in the City of Calgary*. Calgary: Senior Citizens' Central Council of

Calgary. (Also a project submitted to the School of Social Welfare, University of Calgary.)

Gauthier, Pierre
1991   "Canada's Seniors." *Canadian Social Trends*, Autumn:16-20.

Gee, Ellen M.
1990   "Demographic Change and Intergenerational Relations in Canadian Families: Findings and Social Policy Implications." *Canadian Public Policy*, 16:191-199.

Gee, Ellen M., and Meredith M. Kimball
1987   *Women and Aging.* Toronto: Butterworths.

Gee, Ellen M., and Susan A. McDaniel
1993   "Social Policy for an Aging Society." *Journal of Canadian Studies,* 28:139-152.

Gelber, Sylva M.
1980   "The Path to Health Insurance." In C.A. Meilicke and J.L. Storch, (eds.), *Perspectives on Canadian Health and Social Services Policy: History and Emerging Trends.* Ann Arbor, Michigan: Health Administration Press.

Gifford, C. G.
1990   *Canada's Fighting Seniors.* Toronto: Lorimer.

Goffman, Erving
1963   *Stigma: Notes on the Management of Spoiled Identity.* Englewood Cliffs, N.J.: PrenticeHall.

Good, Christopher
1995   "The Generational Accounts of Canada." *Fraser Forum,* August.

Government of Alberta
1996   *Government of Alberta Strategic Business Plan for Alberta Seniors 1996/97 to 1998/99.* In Alberta Community Development, *Alberta Community Development Business Plan and Supplementary Information 1996/97 - 1998/99.* Appendix Three. Pages 17-30. Edmonton.
1988   *Caring and Responsibility: A Statement of Social Policy for Alberta.* Edmonton.

Government of Canada
1996   *The Seniors Benefit: Securing the Future.* Catalogue No. F1-23/1996-4E. Ottawa.
1993   *Ageing and Independence: Overview of a National Survey.* Catalogue No. H88-3/13-1993E. Ottawa: Minister of Supply and Services Canada.
1982   *Canadian Governmental Report on Aging.* Ottawa: Minister of Supply and Services Canada.

Green, Bryan S.
1993   *Gerontology and the Construction of Old Age: A Study in Discourse Analysis.* New York: Aldine de Gruyter.

Gregory, Joy M.
1982   *1982 Seniors Needs Update Survey Report.* Provost and District Family and Community Support Services.

Guallier, Xavier
1982   "Economic Crisis and Old Age: Old Age Policies in France." *Ageing and Society,* 2:165-182.

Guest, Dennis
    1985   *The Emergence of Social Security in Canada.* 2nd edn. rev. Vancouver: University of British Columbia Press.

Guillemard, Anne-Marie
    1983   "The Making of Old Age Policy in France: Points of Debate, Issues at Stake, Underlying Social Relations." In Anne-Marie Guillemard, (ed.), *Old Age and the Welfare State.* Beverly Hills, California: Sage.

Guppy, Neil
    1989   "The Magic of 65: Issues and Evidence in the Mandatory Retirement Debate." *Canadian Journal on Aging,* 8:173-186.

Hancock, Trevor
    1982   "Beyond Health Care," *The Futurist,* (August): 4-13.

Hannochko, Fred (Chairman)
    1974   *Operation New Roof: A Study of the Housing of Senior Citizens in Edmonton.* Edmonton.

Harris, Louis, and Associates, Inc.
    1975   *The Myth and Reality of Aging in America.* Washington, D.C.: The National Council on Aging.

Harrison, Trevor and Gordon Laxer, (eds.),
    1995   *The Trojan Horse: Alberta and the Future of Canada.* Montreal: Black Rose Books.

Havens, Betty
    1980   "Differentiation of Unmet Needs Using Analysis by Age/Sex Cohorts." In V.W. Marshall, (ed.), *Aging in Canada: Social Perspectives.* Don Mills, Ontario: Fitzhenry and Whiteside.

Health Canada
    1994   *Suicide in Canada: Update of the Report of the Task Force on Suicide in Canada.* Catalogue No. H39-107/1995E. Ottawa: Minister of National Health and Welfare.

Health and Welfare Canada
    1993   *Canada's Health Promotion Survey 1990: Technical Report.* Catalogue No. H39-263/2-1990E. Ottawa: Minister of Supply and Services Canada.
    1987a   *Suicide in Canada: Report of the National Task Force on Suicide in Canada.* Ottawa.
    1987b   *The Active Health Report: Perspectives on Canada's Health Promotion Survey 1985.* Ottawa: Minister of Supply and Services Canada.
    1986   *Aging: Shifting the Emphasis* (Summary of Working Paper). Ottawa.
    1982   *Suicide Among the Aged in Canada.* Ottawa.

Henripin, Jacques
    1994   "The Financial Consequences of Population Aging." *Canadian Public Policy,* 20:78-94.

Hertzman, Clyde, and Michael Hayes
    1985   "Will the Elderly Really Bankrupt Us With Increased Health Care Costs?" *Canadian Journal of Public Health,* 76:373-77.

Higham, Brenda
    1988   *Fort Saskatchewan Senior Citizen's Survey: 1988 Final Report.*

Hirdes, John P., and William F. Forbes
    1989   "Estimates of the Relative Risk of Mortality Based on the Ontario Longitudinal Study of Aging." *Canadian Journal on Aging,* 8:222-237.

Hirdes, John P., K.S. Brown, W.F. Forbes, D.S. Vigoda, and L. Crawford
  1986   "The Association Between Self-Reported Income and Perceived Health Based on the Ontario Longitudinal Study of Aging." *Canadian Journal on Aging*, 5:189-204.

Hohn, Nancy
  1986a   *Issues Affecting Older Natives in Alberta – A Discussion Paper*, Edmonton: Senior Citizens Secretariat.
  1986b   *Surveys of Seniors in Alberta*. Edmonton: Senior Citizens Secretariat.

Hull, Eleanor J.
  1979   *An Analytic Comparison of the 1971 and 1976 Studies of Aging in Manitoba: Needs and Resources*. Winnipeg: Manitoba Department of Health.

Institute for Health Care Facilities of the Future
  1988   *Aging: Future Health Care Delivery*. Ottawa.

James, Robert L.
  1964   *Edmonton Senior Residents' Survey Report*. Edmonton: Edmonton Welfare Council.

Jefferys, Margot
  1983   "The Over-Eighties in Britain: The Social Construction of Panic." *Journal of Public Health Policy*, 4:367-372.

Jones, Marion
  1990   "Time Use of the Elderly." *Canadian Social Trends*, Summer:28-30.

Johnson, Malcolm L.
  1995   "Interdependency and the Generational Compact." *Ageing and Society*, 15:243-265.

Keating, Norah C., and Brenda Munro
  1991   *Generations in Alberta Farming Families: Final Report Submitted to the Seniors Advisory Council for Alberta and Alberta Agriculture*. Edmonton.

Keating, Norah, Karen Kerr, Sharon Warren, Michael Grace, and Dana Wertenberger
  1994   "Who's the Family in Family Caregiving?" *Canadian Journal on Aging*, 13:268-287.

Keith, Julie, and Laura Landry
  1992   "Well-being of Older Canadians." *Canadian Social Trends*, Summer:16-17.

Kerr, Janet C., Norma Thurston, Donald E. Larson, and Alfred Rademaker
  1983   "Health Status of the Rural Elderly: Implications for Community Health Nursing Services." In E. Hamrin, (ed.), *Research – A Challenge for Nursing Practice: Proceedings*. Uppsala, Sweden: Swedish Nurses' Association.

Kohn, R.
  1967   *The Health of the Canadian People*. Ottawa: Queen's Printer.

Kraus, Arthur S.
  1988   "Is A Compression of Morbidity in Late Life Occurring? Examination of Death Certificate Evidence." *Canadian Journal on Aging*, 7:58-70.

Krismer, Kirsten
  1982   *A Survey of Independent Seniors in Camrose*.

Lacombe Council on Aging
  1971   *Senior Citizen's Survey: Project Report*.

Lai, Daniel Wing-Leung, and J.R. McDonald
    1995   "Life Satisfaction of Chinese Elderly Immigrants in Calgary."
              Canadian Journal on Aging, 14: 536-552.

Lalonde, Marc
    1974   *A New Perspective on the Health of Canadians.* Ottawa: Government
              of Canada.

LaRocque, Gordie, Cathy Reininger, Mark Holmgren, and Jonathan Murphy.
    1988   *Forgotten Pioneers: A Needs Assessment of Inner City Seniors.*
              Edmonton: Operation Friendship.

Lawrence, R. Paul
    1977   *The County of Strathcona Survey into the Transportation Needs of*
              Senior Citizens and Disabled Persons. County of Strathcona:
              Preventive Social Services.

Leonard, Peter, and Barbara Nichols
    1994   *Gender, Aging and the State.* Montreal: Black Rose Books.

Long Term Care Branch, Alberta Health
    1991   *Residents of Alberta's Long Term Care Facilities: A Descriptive*
              Profile. Edmonton.

Lowe, Graham S.
    1992   "Canadians and Retirement." *Canadian Social Trends,* Autumn:18-21.

Macdonald, P., and K. H. Kurji
    1986   *Health Practices of Edmontonians: A Preliminary Report.* Edmonton:
              Edmonton Board of Health.

Maclean's
    1988   "Revenge of the Cradle." May 30.
    1987   "The New Day Care Policy." December 14.

Maier, Dennis G.
    1975   *Senior Needs Survey Report.* Provost and District Preventive Social
              Services Board.

Manitoba Association on Gerontology
    1983   *Manitoba's Research on Aging: An Annotated Bibliography, 1950-*
              1982. Winnipeg.

Manitoba Department of Health
    1987   *Aging in Manitoba: Needs and Resources, 1983.* Three Volumes.
              Winnipeg.

Manitoba Department of Health and Community Services
    n.d.   *Aging Update 1976.* Winnipeg.

Manitoba Department of Health and Social Development
    1973   *Aging in Manitoba: A Study of the Needs of the Elderly and of*
              Resources Available to Meet Need. Ten Volumes. Winnipeg. Also
              titled *Aging in Manitoba: Needs and Resources 1971.*

Marshall, Victor W.
    1994   "A Critique of Canadian Aging and Health Policy." In V. Marshall and
              Barry McPherson, (eds.), *Aging: Canadian Perspectives.* Peterborough:
              Broadview Press/Journal of Canadian Studies.
    1987a   "Social Perspectives on Aging: Theoretical Notes." In V.W. Marshall,
              (ed.), *Aging in Canada: Social Perspectives,* 2nd edition. Markham,
              Ontario: Fitzhenry and Whiteside.
    1987b   "The Health of Very Old People as a Concern of Their Children." In

V.W. Marshall, (ed.), *Aging in Canada: Social Perspectives*, 2nd edition. Markham, Ontario: Fitzhenry and Whiteside.

Martin, Paul
    1996a   *Budget in Brief.* Ottawa: Department of Finance Canada.
    1996b   *Budget Speech.* Ottawa: Department of Finance Canada.
    1995a   *Budget Speech.* Ottawa: Department of Finance Canada.
    1995b   *Budget in Brief.* Ottawa: Department of Finance Canada.

Marzouk, M. S.
    1991   "Aging, Age-Specific Health Care Costs and the Future Health Care Burden in Canada." *Canadian Public Policy*, 17:490-506.

McBlane, Nan
    1982   "Human Rights and Older Persons: A Discussion Paper Prepared for the Provincial Senior Citizens Advisory Council 1982 Report to the Minister of Social Services and Community Health." Appendix B in Provincial Senior Citizens Advisory Council, *1982 Report*. Edmonton.

McDaniel, Susan A.
    1993   "Emotional Support and Family Contacts of Older Canadians." *Canadian Social Trends*, Spring:30-33.
    1987   "Demographic Aging as a Guiding Paradigm in Canada's Welfare State." *Canadian Public Policy,* 13:330-336.
    1986   *Canada's Aging Population.* Toronto: Butterworths.

McDaniel, Susan A., and Allison L. McKinnon
    1993   "Gender Differences in Informal Support and Coping Among Elders: Findings from Canada's 1985 and 1990 General Social Surveys." *Journal of Women and Aging,* 5:79-98.

McDonald, P. Lynn
    1995   "Editorial: Retirement for the Rich and Retirement for the Poor: From Social Security to Social Welfare." *Canadian Journal on Aging,* 14:447-457.

McDonald, P. Lynn, and Richard A. Wanner
    1990   *Retirement in Canada.* Toronto: Butterworths.

McKinnon, Allison L., and David Odynak
    1991   *Elder Care, Employees, and Employers: Some Canadian Evidence. A Discussion Paper Prepared for the Demographic Review Secretariat, Health and Welfare Canada.* Edmonton, Population Research Laboratory, University of Alberta.

McQ Enterprises
    1986   *A Review of Senior Citizens Surveys in Alberta and Other Provinces.* Edmonton: Senior Citizens Secretariat.

McVey, Wayne W., and Warren E. Kalbach
    1995   *Canadian Population.* Toronto: Nelson.

Mechanic, David
    1978   *Medical Sociology*, 2nd ed. New York: The Free Press.

Medicine Hat Preventive Social Services Department
    n.d.   *Senior Outreach: A Community Study of the Future Expectations and Needs of Retired Persons in Medicine Hat.*

Meilicke, Carl A., and Janet L. Storch (eds.)
    1980   *Perspective on Canadian Health and Social Services Policy: History*

and Emerging Trends. Ann Arbor, Michigan: Health Administration
Press.

Merrett, Kathryn
1986   *Approaches to Surveying Seniors' Issues in Alberta*. Edmonton: Senior
Citizens Secretariat.

Messinger, Hans, and Brian J. Powell
1987   "The Implications of Canada's Aging Society on Social Expenditures."
In V.W. Marshall, (ed.), *Aging in Canada. Social Perspectives*. 2nd
edition. Markham, Ontario: Fitzhenry and Whiteside.

Minkler, Meredith
1983   "Blaming the Aged Victim: The Politics of Scapegoating in Times of
Fixed Conservation." *International Journal of Health Services* ,
13:155-168.

Minkler, Meredith, and Thomas R. Cole
1991   "Political and Moral Economy: Not Such Strange Bedfellows." In
Meredith Minkler and Carroll L. Estes, (eds.), *Critical Perspectives on
Aging: The Political and Moral Economy of Growing Old*. Amityville,
New York: Baywood.

Minkler, Meredith, and Carroll L. Estes, (eds.)
1991   *Critical Perspectives on Aging: The Political and Moral Economy of
Growing Old*. Amityville, New York: Baywood.

Mossey, Jana M., Betty Havens, Noralou P. Roos, and Evelyn Shapiro
1981   "The Manitoba Longitudinal Study on Aging: Description and Methods."
The Gerontologist, 21:551-558.

Munro, Brenda, Norah Keating, and Xiumei Zhang
1995   "Stake in Farm and Family: A Two Generation Perspective," *Canadian
Journal on Aging*, 14: 564-579.

Myles, John F.
1991   "Editorial: Women, the Welfare State, and Care-Giving." *Canadian
Journal on Aging*, 10:82-85.

1989   *Old Age in the Welfare State: The Political Economy of Public Pensions*.
rev. ed. Lawrence, Kansas: University Press of Kansas.

1988   "Social Policy in Canada." In E. Rathbone-McCuan and B. Havens,
(eds.), *North American Elders: United States and Canadian
Perspectives*. New York: Greenwood.

1984   *Old Age in the Welfare State: The Political Economy of Public
Pensions*. Toronto: Little, Brown.

Myles, John, and Jill Quadagno, (eds.)
1991   *States, Labor Markets, and the Future of Old-Age Policy*. Philadelphia:
Temple University Press.

Myles, John, and Debra Street
1995   "Should the Economic Life Course be Redesigned? Old Age Security
in a Time of Transition," *Canadian Journal on Aging*, 14:335-359.

Myles, John, and Les Teichroew
1991   "The Politics of Dualism: Pension Policy in Canada." In John Myles
and Jill Quadagno, (eds.), *State, Labor Markets, and the Future of
Old-Age Policy*. Philadelphia: Temple University Press.

National Council of Welfare
1996a   *Poverty Profile 1994*. Ottawa: Minister of Supply and Services Canada.

1996b   *A Guide to the Proposed Seniors Benefit*. Ottawa: Minister of Supply and Services Canada.

1996c   *A Pension Primer*. Ottawa: Minister of Supply and Services Canada.

1984a   *Sixty-Five and Older: A Report by the National Council of Welfare on the Incomes of the Aged*. Ottawa: Minister of Supply and Services Canada.

1984b   *Better Pensions for Homemakers*. Ottawa: Minister of Supply and Services Canada.

Nessner, Katherine

1990   "Profile of Canadians with Disabilities." *Canadian Social Trends*, Autumn:2-5.

Neysmith, Sheila M.

1987   "Social Policy Implications of an Aging Society." In V.W. Marshall, (ed.), *Aging in Canada: Social Perspectives*, 2nd edition. Markham, Ontario: Fitzhenry and Whiteside.

Neysmith, Sheila, and Joey Edwardh

1983   "Ideological Underpinnings of the World Assembly on Aging." *Canadian Journal on Aging*, 2:125-136.

Norland, J. A.

1994   *Profile of Canada's Seniors*. Statistics Canada Catalogue No. 96-312E. Published by Statistics Canada and Prentice Hall Canada.

North Edmonton Services for People Association

1981   *Seniors in Action Survey*. Edmonton.

Northcott, Herbert C.

1994   "Public Perceptions of the Population Aging 'Crisis'." *Canadian Public Policy*, 20:66-77.

1993   "The Politics of Fiscal Austerity and Threats to Medicare." *Health and Canadian Society*, 1:347-366.

1990   *Public Opinion Regarding the Economic Support of Seniors*. Edmonton Area Series Report Number 67. Edmonton: Population Research Laboratory, Department of Sociology, University of Alberta.

1988a   *Changing Residence: The Geographic Mobility of Elderly Canadians*. Toronto: Butterworths.

1988b   "Health-Care Resources and Extra-Billing: Financing, Allocation, and Utilization." In B.S. Bolaria and H.D. Dickinson, *Sociology of Health Care in Canada*. Toronto: Harcourt, Brace, Jovanovich.

1984   "Widowhood and Remarriage Trends in Canada 1956-1981." *Canadian Journal on Aging*, 3(2):63-78.

1982   "The Best Years of Your Life." *Canadian Journal on Aging*, 1:72-78.

Novak, Mark

1993   *Aging and Society: A Canadian Perspective*. Second Edition. Scarborough: Nelson.

1988   *Aging and Society: A Canadian Perspective*. Scarborough: Nelson.

Nutrition Canada

1973   *Nutrition: A National Priority*. Ottawa: Information Canada.

Ogden, Russel

1994   "The Right to Die: A Policy Proposal for Euthanasia and Aid in Dying." *Canadian Public Policy*, 20:1-25.

Oi Kwan Foundation
  1988   *A Needs Survey of the Chinese Elderly in Calgary 1987: Findings and Discussions*. Calgary.

Olshansky, S. Jay, and A. Brian Ault
  1986   "The Fourth Stage of the Epidemiologic Transition: The Age of Delayed Degenerative Diseases." *Milbank Memorial Fund Quarterly*, 64:355-91.

Omran, A.R.
  1971   "The Epidemiologic Transition: A Theory of the Epidemiology of Population Change." *Milbank Memorial Fund Quarterly*, 49:509-38.

Parakulam, George
  1987a   *Promoting the Health of Albertans: A Study of Practices, Attitudes, and Beliefs Impinging on Chronic Disease Prevention*. Edmonton: Alberta Community and Occupational Health.
  1987b   *Peace River Risk Factor Survey 1986*. Edmonton: Alberta Community and Occupational Health.
  1987c   *Behavioral Health Risk Factors in North Central Alberta*. Edmonton: Alberta Community and Occupational Health.

Parakulam, George, and David Odynak
  1989   *The Prevalence of Healthfulness in Alberta*. Edmonton: Alberta Health.

Pederson, Ann P., Richard K. Edwards, Merrijoy Kelner, Victor W. Marshall, and Kenneth R. Allison
  1988   *Coordinating Healthy Public Policy: An Analytic Review and Bibliography*. Ottawa: Minister of Supply and Services Canada.

Philippon, Donald J., and Sheila A. Wasylyshyn
  1996   "Health-Care Reform in Alberta." *Canadian Public Administration*, 39:70-84.

Podnieks, Elizabeth
  1990   *National Survey on Abuse of the Elderly in Canada: The Ryerson Study*. Toronto: Ryerson Polytechnical Institute.

Poulin, Susan
  1996   "Dual-Pensioner Families," *Perspectives on Labor and Income*, 8 (Autumn):24-29. Published by Statistics Canada, Catalogue No. 75-001-XPE.

Powell, Brian J., and James K. Martin
  1980   "Economic Implications of Canada's Aging Society." In V.W. Marshall, (ed.), *Aging in Canada: Social Perspectives*. Don Mills, Ontario: Fitzhenry and Whiteside.

Premier's Council in Support of Alberta Families, Government of Alberta
  1991   *Forum on Indian and Metis Families*. Edmonton: Government of Alberta.

Prince Edward Island Department of Health and Social Services
  1981   *Towards Meeting the Needs of Senior Citizens in Prince Edward Island: Summary*. Charlottetown.

Regional Interdisciplinary Steering Committee for Geriatric Services in the North Peace River Region
  1986   *A New Beginning: A Review of the Needs of Seniors in the North Peace Region*.

Rempel, John D. (ed.)
    1987   *Annotated Bibliography of Papers, Articles, and Other Documents from the Aging in Manitoba 1971, 1976, 1983 Cross-sectional and Panel Studies.* Winnipeg: Aging in Manitoba Project.

Robertson, Ann
    1991   "The Politics of Alzheimer's Disease: A Case Study in Apocalyptic Demography." In Meredith Minkler and Carroll Estes, (eds.), *Critical Perspectives on Aging: The Political and Moral Economy of Growing Old.* Amityville, New York: Baywood.

Rockwood, Kenneth, Paul Stolee, and Duncan Robertson
    1981   *Long Term Care of the Elderly: Report of the Saskatchewan Health Status Survey of the Elderly.* University of Saskatchewan: Division of Geriatric Medicine.

Romaniuc, Anatole
    1984   *Fertility in Canada: From Baby-boom to Baby-bust.* Ottawa: Statistics Canada.

Roos, Noralou P., Betty Havens, and Charlyn Black
    1993   "Living Longer but Doing Worse: Assessing Health Status in Elderly Persons at Two Points in Time in Manitoba, Canada, 1971 and 1983." *Social Science and Medicine,* 36:273-282.

Roos, Noralou P., Evelyn Shapiro, and Leslie L. Roos
    1987   "Aging and the Demand for Health Services: Which Aged and Whose Demand?" In D. Coburn, et al., (eds.), *Health and Canadian Society: Sociological Perspectives,* 2nd edition. Markham, Ontario: Fitzhenry and Whiteside.

Roos, Noralou P., Patrick Montgomery, and Leslie L. Roos
    1987   "Health Care Utilization in the Years Prior to Death," *The Milbank Quarterly,* 65:231-254.

Roos, Noralou P., Evelyn Shapiro, and Robert Tate
    1989   "Does a Small Minority of Elderly Account for a Majority of Health Care Expenditures?: A Sixteen-year Perspective," *The Milbank Quarterly,* 67:347-369.

Rosenthal, Carolyn J.
    1987   "Aging and Intergenerational Relations in Canada." In V.W. Marshall, (ed.), *Aging in Canada: Social Perspectives,* 2nd edition. Markham, Ontario: Fitzhenry and Whiteside.

Ross, Janet Kerr, Sharon Warren, and Dianne Godkin
    1995   *Adult Day Programs: Maintaining the Health Status and Quality of Life of Alberta's Elderly People in the Community.* Edmonton: Alberta Health.

Rutherford, Donna, Trudy MeijerDrees, and Joyce Elliott
    1985   *The Feasibility of Developing Shared Housing for Seniors in Calgary: A Report to the Development and Outreach Committee of the Lutheran Welfare Society.* Calgary: Lutheran Welfare Society.

Saskatchewan Senior Citizens' Provincial Council
    1983   *Saskatchewan Aging: An Annotated Bibliography on Research in Saskatchewan 1945 to the Present.* Regina.

Sawka, Edward
> 1978   *Alcohol Use Among Edmonton Elderly: A Pilot Survey.* Edmonton: Alberta Alcoholism and Drug Abuse Commission.

Schellenberg, Grant
> 1994   *The Road to Retirement: Demographic and Economic Changes in the 90s.* Ottawa: Canadian Council on Social Development.

Schneider, E.L., and J.A. Brody
> 1983   "Aging, Natural Death, and the Compression of Morbidity: Another View." *New England Journal of Medicine,* 309 (October 6):854-856.

Schwenger, Cope, and John Gross
> 1980   "Institutional Care and Institutionalization of the Elderly in Canada." In V.W. Marshall, (ed.), *Aging in Canada: Social Perspectives.* Don Mills, Ontario: Fitzhenry and Whiteside.

Scitovsky, Anne A.
> 1994   "'The High Cost of Dying' Revisited," *The Milbank Quarterly,* 72:561-591.

Sefton, Judy M., and W. Kerry Mummery
> 1995   *The Well-Being of Seniors in Alberta: An Alberta Perspective on the National Survey on Ageing and Independence.* Edmonton: Alberta Centre for Well-Being.

Seniors Advisory Council for Alberta
> 1995   *Programs for Seniors, 1995.* Edmonton.
> 1993   *Older Albertans 1992.* Edmonton.
> 1991a   *Programs for Seniors, 1991.* Edmonton.
> 1991b   *Older Albertans 1990.* Edmonton.
> 1990   *The Older Aboriginal Population in Alberta.* Edmonton.

Shapiro, Evelyn, and Joseph Kaufert
> 1983   "The Role of International Conferences – A Theoretical Framework." *Canadian Journal on Aging,* 2: 43-49.

Simmons-Tropea, Daryl, and Richard Osborn
> 1987   "Disease, Survival, and Death: The Health Status of Canada's Elderly." In V.W. Marshall, (ed.), *Aging in Canada: Social Perspectives,* 2nd edition. Markham, Ontario: Fitzhenry and Whiteside.

Simon Fraser University Gerontology Research Centre
> 1989   *Annotated Bibliography of B.C. Publications on Aging: 1984-1988.* Simon Fraser University.
> 1984   *Research on Aging in British Columbia: An Annotated Bibliography 1950-1983.* Simon Fraser University.

Smoky River Municipal District, Family Service Bureau, Preventive Social Services
> 1974   *Senior Citizens Survey.*

Smoky River Municipal District, Preventive Social Services
> 1979   *Senior Citizens Survey.*

Snider, Earle L.
> 1976   *Health and Related Needs of the Elderly.* Edmonton: Medical Services Research Foundation of Alberta.
> 1973   *Medical Problems and the Use of Medical Services Among Senior Citizens in Alberta: A Pilot Project.* Edmonton: Medical Services Research Foundation of Alberta.

Soderstrom, Lee
    1978   *The Canadian Health System*. London: Croom Helm.

Special Senate Committee on Euthanasia and Assisted Suicide. Senate of Canada.
    1995   *Of Life and Death*. Catalogue No. YC2-351/1-01E. Ottawa: Minister of Supply and Services Canada.

Spencer, Metta
    1985   *Foundations of Modern Sociology*, 4th edition. Scarborough, Ontario: Prentice-Hall.

Stackhouse, Reginald (Chairman)
    1988   *Human Rights and Aging in Canada: Second Report of the Standing Committee on Human Rights*. Ottawa: Queen's Printer.

Statistics Canada
    1995a   *Profile of Canada's Aboriginal Population*. Catalogue No. 94-325. Ottawa: Minister of Industry, Science, and Technology.
    1995b   *National Population Health Survey Overview 1994-95*. Catalogue No. 82-567. Ottawa: Minister of Industry.
    1994a   *Population Projections for Canada, Provinces and Territories 1993-2016*. Catalogue No. 91-520. Ottawa: Minister of Industry, Science, and Technology.
    1994b   *Selected Characteristics of Persons with Disabilities Residing in Households: 1991 Health and Activity Limitation Survey*. Catalogue No. 82-555. Ottawa: Minister of Industry, Science and Technology.
    1989   *Health and Activity Limitation Survey: Subprovincial Data for Alberta*. Catalogue Number 82611. Ottawa.
    1988   *Causes of Death 1986*. Catalogue No. 84203. Ottawa: Minister of Supply and Services Canada.
    1987   *Health and Social Support, 1985*. General Social Survey Analysis Series. Ottawa: Minister of Supply and Services Canada.
    1980   *Perspectives Canada III*. Ottawa: Minister of Supply and Services.

Statistics Canada and Department of the Secretary of State of Canada.
    1986   *Report of the Canadian Health and Disability Survey 1983-84*. Ottawa: Minister of Supply and Services Canada.

Stephens, Thomas, and Cora Lynn Craig
    1990   *The Well-Being of Canadians: Highlights of the 1988 Campbell's Survey*. Ottawa: Canadian Fitness and Lifestyle Research Institute.

Stolee, Paul, Kenneth Rockwood, and Duncan Robertson
    1982   *The Elderly in the Community: Report II of the Saskatchewan Health Status Survey of the Elderly*. University of Saskatchewan Division of Geriatric Medicine.

Stone, June (Chairman, Steering Committee)
    n.d.   *Elk Point and District Senior Citizens' Survey 1987-88*.

Stone, Leroy O., and Michael J. MacLean
    1979   *Future Income Prospects for Canada's Senior Citizens*. Montreal: Institute for Research on Public Policy.

Stone, Leroy O., and Susan Fletcher
    1986   *The Seniors Boom: Dramatic Increases in Longevity and Prospects for Better Health*. Ottawa: Minister of Supply and Services Canada.
    1980   *A Profile of Canada's Older Population*. Montreal: Institute for Research on Public Policy.

Swartz, Donald
  1987   "The Politics of Reform: Conflict and Accommodation in Canadian
          Health Policy." In D. Coburn, et al., (eds.), *Health and Canadian
          Society: Sociological Perspectives*, 2nd edition. Markham, Ontario:
          Fitzhenry and Whiteside.

Taylor, James E.
  1986   *Starting Point: Final Report of the Hinton Seniors' Needs Assessment
          Survey*. Hinton: Community Services Department.

Taylor, Malcolm G.
  1987   "The Canadian Health-Care System: After Medicare." In D. Coburn, et
          al., (eds.), *Health and Canadian Society: Sociological Perspectives*,
          2nd edition. Markham, Ontario: Fitzhenry and Whiteside.
  1980   "The Canadian Health Insurance Program." In C.A. Meilicke and J.L.
          Storch, (eds.), *Perspectives on Canadian Health and Social Services
          Policy: History and Emerging Trends*. Ann Arbor, Michigan: Health
          Administration Press.

Third Career Research Society
  1976   *Retirement in Alberta: Consumer Report*, Edmonton.

Tindale, Joseph A.
  1991   *Older Workers in an Aging Workforce*. Ottawa: National Advisory
          Council on Aging.

Thurston, Norma, Donald E. Larsen, Alfred W. Rademaker, and Janet C. Kerr
  1982   "Health Status of the Rural Elderly: A Picture of Health." Paper
          presented to the 11th Annual Scientific and Educational Meeting of the
          Canadian Association on Gerontology, Winnipeg, Manitoba, November
          47, 1982.

Torrance, George M.
  1987   "Socio-Historical Overview" and "Hospitals as Health Factories." In D.
          Coburn, et al., (eds.), *Health and Canadian Society: Sociological
          Perspectives*, 2nd edition. Markham, Ontario: Fitzhenry and Whiteside.

Townsend, Peter
  1981   "The Structured Dependency of the Elderly: A Creation of Social Policy
          in the Twentieth Century." *Ageing and Society,* 1:5-28.

United States Bureau of the Census
  1991   *1990 Decennial Census of Population and Housing*. Washington, D.C.

Verbrugge, Lois M.
  1989   "Recent, Present, and Future Health of American Adults." *Annual
          Review of Public Health,* 10:333-361.
  1984   "Longer Life but Worsening Health? Trends in Health and Mortality of
          Middle-Aged and Older Persons." *Milbank Memorial Fund Quarterly/
          Health and Society,* 62:475-519.

Walker, Alan
  1991   "Thatcherism and the New Politics of Old Age." In John Myles and
          Jill Quadagno, (eds.), *State, Labor Markets, and the Future of
          Old-Age Policy*. Philadelphia. Temple University Press.
  1983   "Social Policy and Elderly People in Great Britain: The Construction of
          Dependent Social and Economic Status." In Anne-Marie Guillemard,
          (ed.), *Old Age and the Welfare State*. Beverly Hills, California: Sage.
  1981   "Towards a Political Economy of Old Age." *Ageing and Society,*
          1:73-94.

Wilkins, Kathryn
    1996   "Causes of Death: How the Sexes Differ." *Canadian Social Trends*,
            Summer:11-17.

Wilson, Michael H.
    1991   *The Budget Speech*. Ottawa: Department of Finance Canada.
    1990   *The Budget*. Ottawa: Department of Finance Canada.

Zoerb, Bessie
    1983   *Report on the P.E.P. (Priority Employment Program) Project Geriatric
            Identification Program: Minburn-Vermilion Health Unit.*

PRINTED AND BOUND
IN BOUCHERVILLE, QUÉBEC, CANADA,
BY MARC VEILLEUX IMPRIMEUR INC.
IN APRIL, 1997